Teri's Gluten-Free & Grain-Free Healthy Recipes
by Teri Paradiso

Printed in Canada by
Gateway Rasmussen
www.cookbookprinter.com

Photographs by Teri Paradiso and Chiván Paradiso

Photograph on Cover:
Chiván's children and Teri's grandchildren
Donivan and Chianne

Email: paradisoteri@yahoo.com
Website: www.glutenandgrainfreesolutions.com

ISBN: 978-0-615-81159-8

Library of Congress Control Number 2013915475

MOM

*I dedicate this book to you.
It is my pleasure to stand by you, as you have always stood by me.
You made raising six children look effortless, and you did it with love and validation.
I know you have sacrificed precious moments in your life, for my happiness.
You have always believed in my dreams, and you are the source of my inspiration.
I was truly blessed the day I was born,
And God gave you...to me.
I Love You.*

Introduction

Many today are choosing to follow a gluten-free, and, more importantly, a grain-free lifestyle. There are varied reasons for their choices.

For those individuals who refrain from wheat, it may be due to a wheat allergy. Wheat is one of the eight most common food allergies in the United States. A wheat allergy is not an auto-immune disease, and should not be confused with celiac disease. A wheat allergy is an overreaction of the immune system to one or more of the proteins found in wheat. When the wheat is ingested, it can trigger an allergic reaction that may include a range of symptoms from mild to severe. People who are allergic to wheat often may tolerate other grains, unless they are allergic to them also.

Celiac (see-lee-ak) disease is an auto-immune disease, triggered by foods or products containing gluten. Gluten is a protein found in wheat, barley, rye and sometimes, oat. Oat may be processed in facilities that process gluten, therefore, look for gluten-free oat. Celiac disease affects the small intestine and is caused by an abnormal immune reaction to gluten. Celiac disease can cause serious complications, including intestinal damage, and malnutrition. There is a test to determine if you have celiac disease.

Another reason some individuals may refrain from gluten is due to being gluten intolerant, or gluten sensitive. This is not the same as celiac disease. For these individuals, there is no test, as yet. They would be wise to be in tune to their bodies and notice if they have any symptoms when they consume gluten. Both groups would refrain from gluten. What concerns me is that many gluten-free individuals are eating other grains that are not healthy, just because they don't contain gluten. One example is corn flour and products that contain corn. Most corn is contaminated and genetically modified (GMO). In my opinion grain-free is the better choice.

Some individuals refrain from all grains because their symptoms, from a variety of illnesses, have been alleviated. And still others, already following a healthy, grain-free lifestyle, continue to do so because they report to have more energy, happiness, weight loss, mental acuity, emotional balance, and physical endurance.

i

The recipes in this book are the convergence of my love of delicious food, and my dedication to a healthy lifestyle. Good taste should not be sacrificed for a healthy lifestyle, and the recipes that follow are proof of this.

My mission is to transform traditional recipe favorites such as pizza, chicken fingers, cakes, brownies, pies, and other classics into grain-free versions that taste like, or even better than, the originals. There are one hundred and twenty two, great tasting recipes on the following pages.

I try to live by the quote of Hippocrates, the father of medicine, "Let food be your medicine and let medicine be your food." This philosophy is what I will present to you in my recipes.

I truly hope my recipe book will be your loyal companion, on your journey to a healthy lifestyle.

The field of nutrition is ever changing as new information is discovered. I am not a licensed nutritionist. I am a mother, grandmother, (see my grandchildren, Donivan & Chianne on the front cover), and a certified fitness instructor, who has dedicated her life to health and fitness. I stay current on information pertaining to health, fitness, and nutrition. I am sharing with you the information I gathered from my own research, for myself and my family. This research has led me to write this book. I do feel that knowledge can set one free. Please use any of the information in this book, and disregard any information you may not agree with. Most of all, always stay current, and research for yourself.

Taste buds are relative. If your taste buds get used to overly processed foods, trans fats, and refined sugars, it becomes harder for you to taste the natural flavors of the food you eat. The good news is, it doesn't take long for your taste buds to adjust when you begin to eat right. As a society, we have become accustomed to the taste of overly processed foods. I remember when there were but a few different processed foods on the supermarket shelves. Today there are thousands to choose from and most contain high amounts of sugar, chemicals, and other unhealthy ingredients, yet, few or no whole foods. Most of the ingredients, we cannot even pronounce.

Subliminal messages are hidden in the marketing strategies, and we have fallen victim to these messages. They have contributed to obesity and major health problems we see today. We do not need to be victims to these subliminal messages. It's time to take our power and logic back. We need to make better decisions for our health and lifestyle, as well as, for our children and family members.

I am dedicated to helping people understand they can and should make choices that can free them from unnecessary doctor visits, pain, and illness. How many times have you been to a doctor's office and the doctor told you he didn't know the cause of your illness. Yes, he did have a special pill for your symptoms, but maybe not a cure for your illness. Every medication has side effects and may contribute to your next illness, for which there will be another pill. "Exactly, which nutrients are there in medications?" I ask.

It's a fact that we need to take responsibility for our own health. Responsibility simply means, the ability to respond, and we are all capable of that, right? The following recipes will use whole foods, not chemicals, will be easy to make, and they will taste great. Once they are made you will be eating tasty, healthy, homemade foods. Eat well and feel great. We are what we eat, digest and assimilate...is a truth.

Many may not know the different names of grains so I have made a list of some common grains on the following page. Also, please note, three recipes include quinoa pasta. I will note this on the page of each recipe. Quinoa is not a grain, although, the manufacturers have added a little rice flour to the quinoa, to form the pasta. Rice is gluten-free. Some brands add corn flour, which is also gluten-free, but may be genetically modified (GMO). If you make it at all, may I suggest, you buy the rice instead of corn.

GRAINS THAT WILL NOT BE USED IN THIS COOKBOOK

GRAINS: Common grains that **WILL NOT** be used in this cookbook are; WHEAT which includes, SPELT, EMMER, FARRO, EINKORN, KAMUT, and DURUM. RICE (Note: see above). CORN, and any form of corn; Popcorn, corn flour, high fructose corn syrup, corn by other names hidden in ingredients; example: maltodextrin, which is a food additive, may be derived from corn. OATS, BARLEY, RYE, MILLET, WILD RICE, TRITICALE, SORGHUM and TEFF.

PSEUDO-GRAINS

Pseudo-grains act like grains but are not grains. Pseudo-grains are referred to as false grains for this reason. Most of these come from the seeds of broadleaf plants, and are not considered a true grain. Pseudo-grains can and may be used in the recipes. Pseudo-grains do not contain gluten. These pseudo-grains can be found as flour, and/or, in their natural grain-like form, from which you can make cereals, or use as a rice substitute. You can find them in your supermarket or your local health food store.

AMARANTH (a-mah-ran-th): is a staple of the Mayans and the Aztecs. Amaranth has a nut-like flavor, and contains high quality protein, high levels of iron, phosphorous, magnesium, folic acid and the amino acid, lysine. Amaranth adds texture and flavor to bread recipes but needs to be mixed with other flours. Amaranth can be made as hot cereal and tastes similar to cream of wheat or farina.

QUINOA (KEEN-wa): provides high quality protein, providing 8 of the essential amino acids; potassium, folic acid, B vitamins, vitamin A, calcium and vitamin E. Quinoa tastes like a mild corn and bean flavor. Great in breads, stews, salads, and baking. Quinoa is also a great rice substitute.

BUCKWHEAT: Although the name buckwheat implies that it is related to wheat, it is not. It is a broadleaf crop in the same family as rhubarb and sorrel. Buckwheat is a nutritional powerhouse and has a high content of fiber, protein, minerals and vitamins B1 and B2.

FLAXSEED: Flaxseed provides essential nutrients, including protein, essential fatty acids, vitamins and minerals. Flaxseed also contains both soluble and insoluble dietary fiber. Flaxseed adds a pleasant, nutty flavor to baked products. Although rare, some people may have an allergy to flaxseed, so begin by adding very little at first.

CHIA SEED: Chia seeds are rich in protein, minerals, fiber, and calcium. The high content of omega 3's in chia seeds help build new cells, support heart health, as well as, beautiful skin and nails.

OTHER FLOURS GLUTEN-FREE AND GRAIN-FREE

ALMOND FLOUR: Almond flour is a great flour in so many baking recipes. It is one of the most moist and delicious grain-free flours. It is high in protein and low in carbohydrates and sugars. Almond flour has cholesterol lowering effects, and high antioxidant effects of vitamin E. It is high in potassium and magnesium.

COCONUT FLOUR: Coconut flour has the highest percentage of dietary fiber than any other flour. It is also high in protein. By including coconut flour in your baking recipes, you can turn them into delicious, guilt-free, health promoting foods. Ideal for those who follow a low carbohydrate eating plan.

TAPIOCA FLOUR: Produced from the starch of the cassava plant, tapioca flour is used to thicken products such as pudding, starches and gravy. It's a great substitute for corn starch, which is not used in my recipes. It plays a more subtle role in baked products such as muffins, biscuits and other baked goods. Tapioca is very clean in flavor, therefore, does not mask other flavors used. Note that tapioca loses its thickening properties with long cooking or in high acidic conditions. If using for thickening, always add tapioca to cool mixtures and then add to the hot liquid.

ARROWROOT FLOUR: Arrowroot, like tapioca, is used mostly as a thickening agent in soups and gravies. Again, a great substitute for corn starch which is not used in my recipes. Always add arrowroot to cool mixtures and then add to the hot liquid. As the liquid begins to thicken, remove from heat to prevent reversal. As fast as it thickens, it can just as fast become thin again.

SUGAR

Sugar has been known to contribute to many diseases such as cancer, diabetes, obesity, etc. Although some sugars may be natural, sugar in any form, should be limited.

ARTIFICIAL SWEETENERS: Avoid artificial sweeteners. They are not natural and the body does not recognize them. They may cause cancer and other illnesses. They will not be included in the recipes.

TABLE SUGAR (SUCROSE): About half of the sucrose is produced by sugar beets. The other half is produced by sugar cane. Unless the ingredients say "pure cane sugar", they are usually mixed together. Sugar beets are genetically modified, (GMO). It's more difficult to genetically modify sugar cane, but they are working on doing that, with a targeted date of 2015. Table sugar is processed and refined. I will not include table sugar in the recipes.

STEVIA: Stevia is a natural sugar made from a plant. Stevia is much sweeter than sugar. Example: 1 cup sugar = 1 tsp. stevia. Need to acquire a taste for it but it's worth it. Read ingredients to be sure they are not adding other sweeteners. Stevia comes in a liquid and a powder. You can mix in the recipes, half stevia and half honey for better taste, or at least, until you acquire a taste for the stevia. As you get more used to the stevia, change the recipes to include more stevia and less xylitol and honey. I will include stevia in the recipes.

XYLITOL: Xylitol can also be used in recipes, or half xylitol in recipes, with half stevia or honey. Xylitol is equal amount to sugar. Example: 1 tsp. sugar = 1 tsp. xylitol. Xylitol is considered natural but I believe it is slightly processed, so limit the amount you use. Xylitol, being a sugar alcohol, can have a laxative effect in large amounts. Also, xylitol may be made from corn or birchwood, so choose birchwood if you choose to use it at all. Xylitol should not be given to dogs or pets. Xylitol has been promoted as a help, in preventing dental cavities and oral bacteria in the mouth. Xylitol tastes very much like sugar. I will use xylitol in the recipes, in limited amounts.

HONEY: Honey contains antioxidants, enzymes, amino acids, vitamins and minerals. Honey can be mixed with half xylitol or stevia. Honey, although high in nutrients, is still a sugar, and should be limited. I will include honey in the recipes.

FRUITS: Fruits are beneficial due to the nutrient value and fiber content in them, but they are still high in sugar. More often, choose fruits that are low on the glycemic index. Granny smith apples and berries are good choices. Fruits will be used in the recipes.

CAROB

All the chocolate recipes in this book are made using carob. Carob does NOT contain caffeine. Cocoa and chocolate contain caffeine.

CAFFEINE, SUGAR & CHILDREN

Many of us may be sensitive to caffeine and don't even recognize that we are. "Why are we raising our children on sugar and caffeine?" Caffeine is in products that are made from cocoa, such as chocolate, hot chocolate, cupcakes, chocolate milk, candies, ice cream, etc. Caffeine and theobromine in cocoa are both stimulants.

If we take the sugar and caffeine out of our children's diets, maybe some children would not be so hyper-active, nor, have such short attention spans. I am saddened to hear how many children are on medications for attention deficit disorder (ADD) and similar diagnosis. What if all they needed was a change in their diet. Let's not underestimate our foods. Our food choices can be our medicine or our poison. Children will not be deprived if they don't have refined sugar and caffeine, and they will thank you later. If they are raised with healthy foods, their taste buds will be able to taste the natural flavors in those foods. They will actually prefer, and choose natural tasting foods for themselves. Parents set the standards for which their children will come to appreciate. We are their primary role models. It doesn't get more powerful than that. Our children are more influenced by what we do, than what we tell them to do.

OIL

Coconut oil, olive oil and grapeseed oil are all good choices. Coconut oil can stand high heat more than most oils, therefore, it is a great oil for cooking. Coconut oil has a slight sweet taste. Coconut oil is also anti-bacterial, anti-fungal, and has many other health benefits. Always buy organic, expeller-pressed, unrefined coconut oil. Also, buy organic, extra-virgin olive oil, and organic expeller-pressed, unrefined grapeseed oil.

SUGGESTIONS AND TIPS

Peanuts are known to be a highly allergic food and won't be included in the recipes.

Baking soda will be used in the recipes. Buy aluminum-free baking soda.

Baking powder may contain corn, as well as aluminum, therefore, will not be included in the recipes.

Buy alcohol-free extracts.

Organic foods and products should have no radiation, no antibiotics, no synthetic hormones, no GMO's, and no pesticides. Always read the labels.

When possible, buy organic fruits, vegetables and herbs.

When possible, buy organic grass fed beef, wild caught fish, organic free range poultry, and organic free range eggs.

A substitute for soy sauce is coconut aminos. Much of soy is genetically modified, (GMO).

Avoid yeast. Yeast helps bread to rise and may contribute to inflammation in your body.

To cut down on odors when cooking cabbage and cauliflower, add a little vinegar to the water, and don't overcook.

To keep hot oil from splattering, add a little salt to the pan before frying.

Store flours and nuts in freezer if not using right away.

It's best to store baked products in the refrigerator or freezer, if not eating them right away. You can pre-slice, and wrap in parchment paper. I usually wrap some for the refrigerator and some for the freezer. You are baking with natural products, unlike the stores. Stores include chemicals and unhealthy ingredients to lengthen the shelf life. Isn't homemade the best !!

Eating out should be a pleasurable experience. You can bring your bread, dressings, etc. as I do. This is a lifestyle.

Always pre-heat oven before baking.

If you do not have a food processor, you can use a high powered blender for the recipes.

EXERCISE

Exercise a little every day to keep your spine flexible, joints mobile, digestion healthy, and every organ and system in your body working efficiently. Exercise also helps you to release toxins that may contribute to poor health. We all have toxins from food, water, air, products and environment. It's also great for your lymphatic system. Unlike your heart that has a pump, your lymphatic system depends on breath and movement to activate and do it's job. It will keep you healthy and remove toxins. If you are not used to exercise, begin with ten minutes and build from there. Ten minutes will still give you benefits, and may inspire you to do more.

WATER

Water is the fountain of youth. Water is vital to facilitate every body process. You should at least drink 8 ounces of pure water each day. A better rule of thumb may be to drink half your body weight in ounces. A little lemon in your water may contribute to cleansing your liver and help alkalize your system.

MEDITATION

Meditation is a *scientific* process, as well as, a *spiritual* experience. For me, spiritually, prayer is my speaking to God, through his son, and meditation is quieting my mind enough, to listen for his guidance. Scientifically, meditation involves slowing down the frequency of your brain wave pattern. A vehicle is used to do this such as your breath, word, or phrase. Your brain wave pattern is a reflection of the state of consciousness you are in at any given moment. The frequency (speed), is measured by cycles per second. Your mental state is determined by the particular configuration of the four different categories of brain waves; beta, alpha, theta, and delta. Beta being the fastest and delta, the slowest. Theta brain waves are prominent in meditation.

As your brain wave frequencies slow down, their strength progressively becomes greater. Instead of working in small, scattered, fast moving groups, they are freed up to join together, for maximum efficiency. A natural healing takes place, which radiates from the depth of your being to your physical level. Meditation calms your mind and emotions; lowers your blood pressure; enhances your immune system; balances your hormones; increases your energy; increases stamina and endurance; sharpens your mental focus; improves sleep, and brings you to a state of deep and profound peace and wellbeing. The benefits of meditation become infused in your cellular memory, and part of your daily life.

You don't need to be formal to meditate. Just find a comfortable position to sit in. Ideally your spine is erect. Close your eyes and use a focus for the process. It may be, as simple as following your breath, or, a word that brings calm to you, such as peace. Just sit as an observer, a witness, not judging in any way. If thoughts come in....notice....and then bring your attention back to your breath. Try to sit for ten to twenty minutes. Meditation is far from an escape, it is an illumination of reality. Information on my meditation cd is at the back of this book.

CIRCADIAN RYTHMS

Circadian rhythms pertain to rhythmic cycles recurring at approximately 24-hour intervals. They refer to your biological processes that are aligned with nature. The more you align yourself with these rhythms, the healthier you will be, physically, emotionally, psychologically, and spiritually.

Basically speaking, it's best to wake up as early as 6 a.m. During this morning cycle, between the hours of 6 a.m. and 10 a.m., is the best time to have some quiet time for yourself, for prayer, meditation, exercise, and to eat a healthy breakfast.

Between the hours of 10 a.m. and 2 p.m. is when your metabolic fire is at its highest. Therefore, between these hours, you may want to eat your heaviest meal, so you will be able to metabolize it easily.

Between the hours of 2 p.m. and 6 p.m. is a great time to be physically active, and intellectually stimulated. It's good to eat dinner at around the 6 to 7 o'clock hour, and dinner should be a light meal.

Between the hours of 6 p.m. and 10 p.m., you should be winding down from your day. It's natural to see a drop in cortisol and a rise in melatonin in the evening. During this time you may want to engage in calming, restful activities, preparing yourself for sleep. It's best to refrain from eating at least 2 to 3 hours before bedtime.

Getting to sleep by 10 p.m. is ideal, and you most likely will have a restful, deep, sleep. In the morning you should feel wide awake, refreshed, and happy to greet your day.

Between the hours of 10 p.m. and 2 a.m., your stomach secretes digestive acids, which are 2 to 3 times more, than any other time during the day. This may be a cleansing process, and eating late may interfere with this process.

There are three sleep stages. Stage one, drowsiness, is a transitional stage, when you go from wakefulness to light sleep. Stage 2 is a deep sleep, when your body heals and renews itself. The third stage, REM, is when your dreams occur. The REM stage also renews your mind and facilitates learning and memory.

As you follow these simple laws of nature, you will notice your life changing for the better, in every way. Health is not just the absence of disease; it's being in great health, having an abundance of energy, clarity of mind, inner joy, and a zest for life.

FOOD ROTATION

Food rotation, generally speaking, is simply not eating the same foods every day. This refers to all food groups. Research has shown that most individuals basically eat the same 12 foods most of the time. If this is true, it would be difficult to get all the different nutrients that you need. Food rotation may be worth exploring for you and your family. When you eat the same foods every day, it's easy to build up intolerance to those foods, which may eventually have an adverse effect on your health. Also, eating fruits and vegetables in season, from your area and region, is a healthy choice. Of course, always eat organic when you can.

A RAINBOW OF COLORS

A rainbow of colors is a healthy way to think about your fruits and vegetables. In fact, why not try to make salad your staple meal. With such a variety of items to put in a salad, you can make your salad suitable for any meal. Salads make great staple meals, especially in the summer, when you may want something lighter. You can begin with your green leafy vegetables and build from there. Your salad is your creation. It's a guarantee that you will eat your daily allowance of fruits and vegetables. Adding a little fat and protein, such as meat, fish, cheese, nuts, seeds, or hard boiled eggs, will also help to satiate your appetite. The meat or fish can also be served hot for a warmer meal.

There are a rainbow of colors to choose from, and each color represents different nutrients, and health benefits. I have listed some of the nutrients and benefits associated with each color, below.

RED fruits and vegetables, such as beets, cherries, red apples, red onions, and tomatoes, contain nutrients such as lycopene, ellagic acid, quercetin, and hesperidin. These nutrients may help lower blood pressure, reduce the risk of prostate cancer, and help support joint tissue.

ORANGE/YELLOW fruits and vegetables, such as butternut squash, cantaloupe, carrots, lemons, and yellow and orange peppers, contain beta-carotene, zeaxanthin, flavoinoids, potassium and vitamin C. These may reduce age-related macular degeneration, promote collagen formation, and help fight harmful free radicals.

GREEN fruits and vegetables such as artichokes, avocados, broccoli, green peppers and kiwi, contain chlorophyll, fiber, lutein, zeaxanthin, calcium, folate, and beta-carotene. These may reduce cancer risks, support healthy digestion, and boost immune system activity.

BLUE/PURPLE fruits and vegetables such as blackberries, eggplant, plums, grapes, and raisins; contain such nutrients as resveratrol, vitamin C, fiber, flavonoids, and quercetin. These may support retinal eye health, lower cholesterol, build up the cardiovascular system, and fight inflammation.

WHITE fruits and vegetables such as turnips, white peaches, garlic, onions, ginger, and cauliflower, contain beta-glucans, and lignans. These nutrients may activate natural killer B and T cells, helping to reduce the risk of several cancers, and balance hormone levels.

Maybe now, taking a trip to the produce department may have a whole new meaning for you. It may give you a reason to try some fruits and vegetables, you normally wouldn't eat.

BREATH

We can live weeks without food, days without water, and only minutes without breath. Even so, we spend so little time aware of our breath. Our breath mirrors our state of mind. When we are anxious, or stressed, our breath tends to be fast and shallow. When we are calm and relaxed, our breath tends to be slow and deep.

Take a few moments each day to sit quietly and observe your breath. Close your eyes, and without judgment, simply bring your attention to your breath. See if you can make your exhalations just a little longer than your inhalations, without forcing it in any way. After the exhalation, pause, and then take breath in again. You may feel a calmness coming over you, and notice your state of mind is more relaxed and content. You will reap many benefits for a few moments a day, which will be far reaching. From your relationship with yourself, to those you love; to your relationship with your environment, and your world.

RE-ACTIVE OR PRO-ACTIVE

When it comes to food, or any decision for that matter, you have a choice of how you will respond. What happens to you in your life is 10% and how you respond to it is 90%. It's a matter of being re-active or pro-active. Between stimulus and response there is a space, and in that *space* of time, you can choose *how* you will respond. I would like to inspire and impress upon you, to choose to be pro-active. Choosing to have this win/win attitude assures that your decisions are mutually beneficial for all concerned. After all, your decisions rarely affect you alone. Everyone around you, from family, loved ones, to co-workers, may be affected by your decisions.

Food affects every part of your being; mental, physical, emotional, and spiritual. When one part of your being is affected by anything, *good or bad*, this connection will affect the other parts of you, as well. Eating healthy assures that you are doing the best you can for yourself and those you love. May your new healthy lifestyle help you to experience a state of peace, harmony, vitality, happiness, balance, and improved health.

Enjoy the recipes and the journey.

Teri Paradiso

CATEGORY INDEX

My Favorite Recipes

Name of Recipe	Page #

CONVERSION OF PAN AND UTENSIL SIZES

UTENSIL	Measure (Volume)	Measure (cm)	Measure (inches)
Baking or cake pan	2 L	20 cm square	8-inch square
	2.5 L	23 cm square	9-inch square
	3 L	30x20x5	12x8x2
	3.5 L	33x21x5	13x9x2
Cookie sheet		40x30	16x12
Jelly roll pan	2 L	40x25x2	15x10x3/4
Loaf pan			
Round layer cake pan	1.2 L	20x4	8x1-1/2
			9x1-1/2
Pie pan	750 mL	20x3	8x1-1/4
	1 L	23x3	9x1-1/4
Tube pan	2 L	20x7	8x3
	3 L	23x10	9x4
Springform pan	2.5 L	23x6	9x3
	3 L	25x8	10x4
Baking dish	1 L		1 qt.
	1.5 L		1-1/2 qt.
	2 L		2 qt.
	2.5 L		2-1/2 qt.
	3 L		3 qt.
	4 L		4 qt.
Custard cup	200 mL		6 fl. oz.
Muffin pans	40 mL	4x2.5	1.5x1
	75 mL	5x3.5	2x1-1/4
	100 mL	7.5x3.5	3x1-1/2
Mixing bowls	1 L		1 qt.
	2 L		2 qt.
	3 L		3 qt.

PAN-SEARED SPICY ARTICHOKE LEAVES WITH PINE NUTS

2 large artichokes
1/2 tsp. lemon juice
2 tbsp. olive oil
6 garlic cloves, minced
1 onion, finely chopped
1/2 c. pine nuts

1/2 tsp. salt
1/2 tsp. garlic powder
1/2 tsp. cayenne pepper
1/2 tsp. turmeric
1 tbsp. fresh parsley, chopped

Clean and trim the sharp tips from the leaves of the artichokes with a scissor. Pull the leaves off of the artichokes.

Fill a large pot with water. Place artichoke leaves and lemon juice into the water. Bring to boil over medium-high heat. Boil for 10 minutes or until tender. Drain completely to remove excess water. Dry the artichoke leaves.

In a large skillet, heat olive oil over medium heat. Add onions and sauté for one minute. Add garlic and sauté for another minute. Add pine nuts and cook for another minute. Add the dry artichoke leaves and mix together. Mix spices and parsley in a small bowl and combine. Add to skillet.

Lower heat and simmer for 5 more minutes.

JALAPEÑO HUMMUS

1 15 oz. can chickpeas
   (garbanzo beans) drained
2 tbsp. olive oil
1/4 c. tahini
   (sesame seed paste)

1 jalapeño pepper,
   seeded, finely diced
3 tbsp. lemon juice
1/4 tsp. sea salt
2 garlic cloves, minced

Combine all ingredients in a food processor or high powered blender. Process until smooth and creamy. Serve with multi-colored, fresh vegetables, or grain-free crackers.

GUACAMOLE AND TORTILLA CHIPS

Guacamole:

3 Haas avocados, seeded,
   peeled and scooped
1 lime, juiced
1/2 tsp. sea salt
1/2 tsp. ground cumin
1/2 tsp. cayenne

1/2 onion, diced
1 garlic clove, minced
1/2 jalapeño pepper,
   seeded and minced
2 Roma tomatoes,
   seeded and diced
1 tbsp. cilantro, chopped

In a large bowl, mash together the avocados, lime juice, salt, cumin and cayenne. Mix well. Fold in the onion, garlic, jalapeño pepper, tomatoes and cilantro.

If not serving right away, refrigerate.

Chips:

1 c. almond flour
1/8 c. flax seed meal
1/8 c. boiling water
1/2 tsp. sea salt

1/2 tsp. fresh cracked pepper
1/8 tsp. garlic powder
1 tbsp. olive oil

In a medium bowl, combine almond flour, flax seed meal, boiling water, salt, pepper, garlic, and olive oil. Mix well. Divide dough into 4 equal size parts.

Form each into a ball. Use a tortilla press for best results. Place parchment paper on top and bottom of tortilla press. The press will make dough even and thin. You would still follow instructions to cook in the skillet. If you do not have a press, follow the following instructions for rolling dough.

Place each ball in between 2 pieces of parchment paper. Use a rolling pin to roll dough into 6 inch circles.

Heat dry skillet on medium-high heat. Take top parchment paper off tortilla and flip tortilla over and place in skillet. Gently, remove the bottom parchment paper. Cook for 2 to 3 minutes on each side or until golden brown. Repeat with each tortilla. Cut into triangles, and serve with guacamole.

BOATS AND BARRELS
WITH CREAM CHEESE STUFFING

4 oz. cream cheese	**7 celery stalks,**
1 raw red pepper, diced small	**cut in 2 in. pieces**
1/8 tsp. onion powder	**7 extra thick carrots,**
1/4 tsp. onion flakes	**cut in 2 in. pieces**
	14 decorative toothpicks

Soften cream cheese at room temperature. Blend in red pepper, onion powder, and onion flakes. Paprika can also be put into mixture.

Carrots need to be thick enough to use an apple corer to remove the center. Vertically place 2 inch carrot.

Place the corer on top and press down. This will remove the center and leave a barrel shape.

Fill inside celery boats with cream cheese mixture.

Fill inside carrot barrels with cream cheese mixture.

Sprinkle with paprika if you choose. Serve immediately or refrigerate until serving time. Serve with toothpicks.

** Note: Only the thick part of carrot can be used or the apple corer won't fit through to make the barrel.

You can grate up the thin parts of the carrot and add to the cream cheese mixture if you want.

Our minds can occupy only one thought at a time...
make it a happy, healthy one.
- Chiván Paradiso

STUFFED ARTICHOKES

4 large artichokes
1 lemon, sliced in wedges
3 tbsp. olive oil
2 large onions, chopped fine
6 cloves garlic, chopped

3 c. quinoa, cooked,
1 c. uncooked = 3 c. cooked
3 tbsp. fresh parsley, chopped
Salt & pepper to taste
1 tsp. garlic powder

Clean artichokes. Cut off stem just under base so artichoke sits flat and upright. With a knife cut off 1/2 inch from top. With scissors, trim tip of each leaf. Rub outside of artichoke with lemon to keep from browning.

Boil water in steamer. Add artichokes (including stems), cover and cook on medium for 20 minutes or until tender. Done when leaves pull out easily and the base can be pierced with a knife. Drain and chop stems into small pieces.

In large skillet heat 2 tablespoons olive oil on medium heat. Add onions and sauté until translucent. Add garlic and stems; cook for another minute. Add cooked quinoa, parsley and seasonings. Mix together. Continue mixing and turning the quinoa mix until quinoa is brown and crispy. Remove from heat.

Turn each artichoke upside down and tap on cutting board to loosen leaves. Turn back to flat side and open leaves with fingers. Go to center and pull out the fuzzy "choke" and discard.

Fill center with quinoa and then stuff each leaf until all leaves are filled to top.

Sit artichokes flat in large baking pan. Fill with water 1/2 inch.

Drizzle with 1 tablespoon olive oil, and squeeze another wedge of lemon over artichokes.

Bake at 400 F for 20 minutes. Broil for 1 to 2 minutes.

Be sure that as you scramble up the ladder of success,
it is leaning against the right building.
- Stephen Covey

ITALIAN CAPRESE KEBOBS

20 small decorative skewers
  or toothpicks
20 small, fresh, bocconcini
  mozzarella balls
20 fresh basil leaves,
  small and whole

20 grape tomatoes
1/4 c. olive oil
Coarse salt to taste
Freshly ground black pepper
  to taste
Dried basil to sprinkle on top

Thread one mozzarella, basil and tomato on each small skewer, or more if you choose to use a large skewer. Use small basil leaves, but if all you have are large leaves, you can fold them. Put on a serving platter. Repeat until all are done. Drizzle with olive oil, and sprinkle salt, pepper and dried basil.

** You can use cherry tomatoes if you want, although I prefer the taste of the grape tomato.

PIZZA MINI'S

2 c. grated cauliflower
1 c. grated fresh mozzarella
  cheese,
1/4 c. egg whites
1/4 tsp. garlic powder

1/4 tsp. oregano, dried
1/4 tsp. basil, dried
1/2 tsp. sea salt
Tomato sauce or pizza sauce
  for dipping

Cook grated cauliflower in a dry skillet over medium heat. Stir constantly, until soft, for about 6 minutes. Place cauliflower into large bowl. Set aside.

In food processor or high powered blender, mix egg whites, cheese, and seasonings. Add to cauliflower and combine thoroughly.

Line a baking sheet with parchment paper or lightly oiled silicone mat. Use an ice cream scoop or large serving spoon to spoon mini pizzas onto baking sheet. Tap lightly to flatten slightly. Bake at 425 F or 30 minutes. Serve with sauce for dipping or topping.

** To cut down on odors when cooking cauliflower, add a little apple cider vinegar to the water.

SWEET MINI RAISIN MEATBALLS

1 lb. ground beef	1 tsp. pepper
1/8 c. almond flour	1 large egg, beaten
2 cloves garlic, minced	1 c. raisins
1/2 tsp. basil	2 tbsp. olive oil
1/2 tsp. parsley	Salsa (optional), for dipping
1/2 tsp. oregano	Marinara sauce (optional),
1/2 tsp. sea salt	for dipping

In a large mixing bowl, add meat, almond flour, fresh garlic, all the seasonings, and the egg.

Mix with gloves or clean hands until thoroughly combined. Fold in raisins until evenly combined. Form the mixture into 1 inch meatballs.

Heat oil in skillet on medium and add meatballs. Fry and turn until all sides are browned.

Lower heat to simmer, cover and cook for 20 minutes or until thoroughly cooked through. Great just the way they are, or you can serve with side of salsa or marinara sauce.

AVOCADO DIP

1 ripe, peeled and pitted avocado	1/4 c. fresh cilantro
1/2 c. plain Greek yogurt	1 tsp. fresh mint
2 tbsp. lime juice	1 clove garlic
	1/4 tsp. salt

Place all ingredients in a food processor or high powered blender. Blend until smooth.

Serve with any crackers from my recipe book, and/or fresh raw vegetables.

GREEN PRINCESS DIP

1/3 c. onions, finely chopped
1/3 c. fresh parsley
1/3 c. chives, chopped
3 tsp. fresh tarragon, chopped

Juice from 1/2 lemon
Black pepper to taste
1 1/2 c. Greek yogurt

Mix all ingredients (except the yogurt) in a food processor or high powered blender. Blend until it makes a paste. Add the yogurt and process until smooth. Refrigerate until ready to serve.

Serve with all colored veggies and/or with grain-free crackers.

SHRIMP COCKTAIL

Shrimp:

1 lb. peeled, tail-on, raw
   shrimp, cleaned

Lime wedges for garnish
Cocktail sauce (optional)

Bring a large pot of water to boil over medium-high heat. Place shrimp into boiling water. Cook until the shrimp rise to the surface and turn pink. Drain water from shrimp and rinse under cool water. Keep shrimp cold over ice.

Garnish with lime. Serve with cocktail sauce (optional).

Cocktail Sauce:

6 oz. tomato paste
4 tbsp. horseradish

Juice of 1/2 lemon
1/2 tsp. salt

Mix all ingredients in a small bowl. Whisk together until evenly combined.

WINTER CIDERLAND

1 c. apple cider
1/8 tsp. cinnamon
1/8 tsp. nutmeg

Dash of clove
1 cinnamon stick

Heat apple cider on medium heat to just before boiling. Sprinkle in the spices. Add cinnamon stick.

GINGER ALE

1/2 c. water
1/2 c. xylitol
2 (3 in.) pieces of lemon peel

1/3 c. fresh ginger root, peeled and chopped
Club soda or sparkling water

In a small saucepan, over medium-high heat, add the water and xylitol. Stir until xylitol is melted. Add ginger and lemon peel, and reduce heat to low. Simmer for 15 minutes, uncovered. Remove from heat and cover. Allow ginger and lemon to steep until it is cool, about 20 minutes.

Pour syrup through a small strainer to strain out the ginger and lemon peel, reserving the syrup.

Fill a glass with ice. Add about 3 tablespoons of ginger syrup and top with club soda. Stir. Taste and adjust to your preference.

Pour remaining syrup into a glass jar, and store in refrigerator.

You are the master of your thought, the molder of your character and the maker and shaper of condition, environment and your destiny.
- James Allen

HOT PEPPERMINT CAROB

3/4 c. boiling water
1 peppermint tea bag
1/2 c. almond milk, unsweetened

1 tbsp. natural unsweetened carob
Whipped cream (optional)

Pour boiling water over tea bag and allow to steep for 3 minutes. Remove bag. Add carob to tea. Stir to dissolve. Add almond milk to cup. Stir. Add stevia or xylitol to taste. Stir. Can top with whipped cream from cookbook, if you desire.

COCONUT STRAWBERRY SMOOTHIE

1 c. unsweetened, whole coconut milk
6 large strawberries, frozen
Stevia or xylitol to sweeten

Unsweetened shredded coconut (optional)
Whipped cream (optional)
1 large strawberry for the top

Place all ingredients in a high powered blender. Blend until smooth. Stir in shredded coconut if desire. Whipped cream, (optional). Put large strawberry on top.

BLUEBERRY SMOOTHIE

1 c. blueberries, fresh or frozen
1/2 c. plain Greek yogurt
1/2 c. almond milk, unsweetened

Stevia or xylitol, sweeten to taste
Non-dairy whipped cream from book (optional)

Blend all ingredients in a high powered blender until thick and creamy. Top with whipped cream if you desire.

** For a thicker smoothie use frozen blueberries. Can also use strawberries, blackberries, etc. for a different smoothie each time.

EXTRA RECIPES:

_____

_____

_____

_____

_____

_____

_____

_____

_____

_____

_____

_____

_____

_____

_____

Soups & Salads

EQUIVALENTS AND SUBSTITUTIONS

1 pound shelled walnuts	=	3 cups chopped walnuts
1 pound raisins	=	2-3/4 cups seedless raisins
1 pound dates	=	2-1/2 cups pitted dates
1 tablespoon cornstarch	=	2 tablespoons flour or 4 teaspoons tapioca
1 medium clove of garlic	=	1/8 tsp. garlic powder
1 cup honey	=	1 cup molasses or corn syrup
1 cup ketchup	=	1 cup tomato sauce plus 1/2 cup sugar plus 2 tablespoons vinegar
1 teaspoon dry mustard	=	1 tablespoon prepared mustard
1 small onion	=	1 tablespoon dried onion
1 cup tomato juice	=	1/2 cup tomato sauce plus 1/2 cup water
1 cup self-rising flour	=	1 cup flour plus 1-1/2 tablespoons baking powder plus 1/2 teaspoon salt
1 egg	=	1 teaspoon cornstarch
1 cup liquid honey	=	1-1/4 cups sugar plus 1/4 cup liquid
1 cup corn syrup	=	1 cup sugar plus 1/4 cup liquid
1 cup buttermilk	=	1 cup plain yogurt
1 cup sour cream	=	1 cup plain yogurt
1 cup tomato juice	=	1/2 cup tomato paste plus 1/2 cup water

BUTTERNUT SQUASH SOUP

2 c. cubed butternut squash
1 small onion, chopped
2 tbsp. olive oil
4 fresh sage leaves
1/2 c. water

1 Granny Smith apple,
    cored, peeled and chopped
Sprinkle dried sage
1/4 c. chopped walnuts

Heat oil in skillet on medium heat. Add sage leaves and sauté until crisp. Remove sage leaves and discard.

Add butternut squash, onions, apple and water. Lower heat to simmer for 10 minutes or until softened. Put squash mixture into a food processor or high powered blender. Be sure top is secure due to hot mixture. Mix to purée. Put in bowl and sprinkle with dried sage and walnuts.

ESCAROLE AND BEANS SOUP

2 bunches of escarole, ribs
    removed, clean & cut
2 15 oz. cans white cannellini
    beans, with juice
Salt to taste

Garlic powder to taste
2 tbsp. olive oil
3 cloves fresh garlic, chopped
2 tbsp. grated cheese
    (optional)

In a large pot, add escarole and 1 cup of water. Cook on high until it boils. Lower heat to medium. Add garlic powder and salt. Cook for 10 minutes or until almost tender.

Meanwhile, heat olive oil in small pot on medium heat. Add garlic and sauté until slightly browned. Add kidney beans and cook for 5 minutes.

Drain escarole, reserving 1/2 cup of the juice from cooking.

Place escarole and juice in a large serving bowl. Pour beans, garlic and oil over the escarole and mix together. Can top with grated cheese if you like.

HEARTY LENTIL SOUP

12 oz. dry lentils	**1 c. crushed tomatoes**
10 c. water	**1 small bag of spinach,**
1 tbsp. olive oil	**coarsely chopped**
1 large yellow onion, chopped	**1/2 tsp. oregano, dried**
3 large carrots, diced	**Salt to taste**
2 large celery stalks, diced	**1/4 tsp. cayenne pepper**
2 garlic cloves, chopped	

Put lentils in a colander. Sort through the lentils in case there are any stones, etc. Rinse lentils thoroughly.

In a large pot, add lentils and 10 cups of water. (Add more water as needed.) Cook on high until the water boils. Lower to medium and simmer gently with lid tilted.

Meanwhile, heat oil in a large skillet on medium heat. Add onions and cook until translucent. Add carrots and cook for another minute. Mix in celery. Add garlic and cook until fragrant.

Pour in crushed tomatoes, spinach, oregano, salt, and cayenne pepper. Cook for another 2 minutes.

When lentils have been cooking for 30 minutes, add vegetables to the lentil pot. Stir occasionally, until lentils are almost tender, about another 15 minutes.

If someone in your life is a bad influence, remember, you can also learn what not to do, from someone.
- Teri Paradiso

HOMEMADE CHICKEN SOUP

1 dry bayleaf
1 clove garlic
3 sprigs thyme
5 whole black peppercorns
5 chicken breasts, on bone
   or boneless, cleaned
2 medium onions, chopped

1/4 c. chopped fresh parsley
1/2 tsp. garlic powder
1/4 tsp. cayenne pepper
Salt to taste
1 lb. carrots, chopped
1 lb. celery, chopped

In a piece of cheesecloth, place the bay leaf, fresh garlic, thyme and black peppercorns. Tie cheesecloth with kitchen twine.

In a large pot, add chicken, onions, parsley, garlic powder, cayenne pepper, salt and cheesecloth.

Add enough water to cover. Bring to boil over high heat. Reduce to simmer and cook partially covered for 45 minutes or until chicken is cooked through. Skim foam that rises to top and discard. Remove chicken from pot and set aside.

Meanwhile, add carrots. After 5 minutes add celery. Carrots take longer to cook than celery. Be sure not to overcook vegetables.

When chicken is cool enough to handle shred into bite size pieces and return to pot. Cook until heated through.

** You can use a whole chicken if you like dark meat.

Make this soup at the first sign of a sniffle, and see the healing begin.

Treat others with respect and love.
Even if only half return it, it's still worth it.
- Gary Langbaum

SPICY MINESTRONE SOUP

1 tbsp. olive oil
1 c. chopped onions
3 garlic cloves, minced
1 c. peeled and diced carrots
1 c. diced celery
28 oz. can crushed tomatoes
Water from 1/2 can of the
    tomatoes
1 c. white cannellini beans,
    include the liquid

1 c. red cannellini beans,
    include the liquid
2 tbsp. fresh basil
1 tsp. dried oregano
1/4 tsp. salt
1/8 tsp. coarse ground black
    pepper
1/8 tsp. cayenne pepper
2 c. diced zucchini
2 tbsp. Parmesan cheese
    (optional)

Heat oil in a large saucepan over medium-high heat. Add onion and cook until translucent. Add garlic and cook another minute. Add carrots and celery; cook for 3 minutes. Pour in tomatoes and water. Add beans and spices. Mix all ingredients together and bring to a boil.

Lower heat to simmer and add zucchini. Cover pot with lid, 3/4 of the way, and cook for 30 minutes, stirring occasionally. Top with Parmesan cheese if you desire.

SUMMER-TIME SALAD

1 large cucumber, chopped
1 can chick peas,
    drained and washed
1 can black olives,
    drained and washed
1 small onion,
    sliced thin and chopped

2 cloves garlic, minced
2 vine ripe tomatoes, chopped
1 tsp. dried oregano
Sea salt to taste
Fresh cracked pepper to taste
1/3 c. olive oil

In a large, chilled serving bowl, add all ingredients (except oregano, salt, pepper, and oil). Mix to combine. Add oregano, salt, pepper and oil. Toss gently.

AVOCADO AND GARBANZO BEAN SALAD

1 large bag of field greens	1/2 red onion, diced
1 cucumber, peeled and chopped	1 tomato, chopped
1/2 can black olives	1/4 c. chopped celery
1/2 can garbanzo beans (chickpeas)	Salt to taste
1/2 avocado, chopped	Garlic powder to taste
	1 tsp. oregano

Mix all ingredients in a large, chilled bowl.

Toss in avocado dressing.

Avocado Dressing:

1 ripe avocado, peeled & pitted	1 tbsp. lime juice
1 clove garlic	1/3 c. olive oil
	1/4 c. fresh basil leaves

Place all ingredients in a food processor or high powered blender. Process until smooth.

CAPRESE SALAD

1/2 lb. fresh mozzarella, 1/4 in. thick slices	25 fresh basil leaves, whole
2 large vine-ripe tomatoes, 1/4 in. thick slices	Salt to taste
	Fresh ground pepper to taste
	1/4 c. olive oil, for drizzling

Alternate layers of tomato, mozzarella and basil in a circular design around a serving plate. Begin with tomato, then basil leaf, and finally, mozzarella.

Continue this way until the plate is covered. Be sure not to hide the basil as it is smaller than the tomato and mozzarella.

Season with salt and pepper. Drizzle the salad with olive oil.

CAESAR SALAD
WITH CRUNCHY CROUTONS

Croutons:

4 slices of my almond flour
    bread (see recipe)
3 tbsp. olive oil
1 tsp. garlic powder

1/2 tsp. cracked pepper
1/4 tsp. dried rosemary
    (optional)

Cut bread into cubes, about (2x2 cm). Place cubes into a large bowl. Pour oil in bowl and lightly coat all sides of cubes. Sprinkle all sides with spices.

Line a baking sheet with parchment paper or a silicone mat. Put cubes in the pan, in a single layer. Bake at 350 F for 5 to 8 minutes. Watch closely, turning and browning on all sides. Done when golden brown and crunchy.

Dressing:

2 anchovy fillets (optional)
1 clove garlic, minced
1/4 c. cashews
1 tbsp. apple cider vinegar
1 tbsp. lemon juice
1 tbsp. mustard, made with
    apple cider vinegar

1/3 c. olive oil
1/2 zucchini,
    peeled, and chopped
1/4 c. grated Parmesan or
    asiago cheese

Use a small mini food processor, or whisk, to mince anchovy and garlic together. If not using anchovy you can add garlic with other ingredients.

Add remaining ingredients and process until smooth. Put in container and refrigerate until serving. The longer the dressing is chilled, the more the flavors will blend together.

Salad:

1 large bunch romaine lettuce,
    shred thin and bite size

1 tbsp. grated Parmesan
    cheese or asiago cheese

Put lettuce in a large serving bowl. Add dressing, and toss until well combined. Sprinkle extra cheese on top if you choose. Top with crunchy croutons.

CUCUMBER SALAD
WITH MINT DRESSING

Salad:

1 large bag of field greens, chopped

1 medium cucumber, peeled and chopped

5 fresh mint leaves, chopped

1/2 c. black olives, sliced

1 medium avocado, peeled and sliced,

1/4 red onion, sliced very thin

1 c. red grapes, sliced

1/4 c. sunflower seeds

Sea salt, to taste

Ground black pepper, to taste

Mix all ingredients in a chilled large serving bowl. Pour dressing on salad and toss.

Cucumber Mint Dressing:

1 medium cucumber, peeled and diced

6 oz. plain Greek yogurt

10 fresh mint leaves, chopped

1/2 tsp. lime juice

1 garlic clove, minced

Place all ingredients in a blender. Blend until puréed. Pour onto salad and toss until thoroughly combined.

** Can use this dressing as a dip also.

*No one has greater love than this,
that he lay down his life for his friends.
- John 15:13*

NO-MAYO SLAW

2 Granny Smith apples,
cored, sliced julienne style
2 limes, juiced
1 tbsp. mustard
2 tbsp. olive oil
2 tbsp. honey
1/2 tsp. sea salt
1/2 head purple cabbage,
shredded

1 carrot,
peeled, sliced julienne
7 large radishes,
sliced julienne
1/4 c. fresh dill,
finely chopped
1/4 c. fresh cilantro,
finely chopped

In a chilled, large serving bowl, add apples. Add enough lime juice, to coat so apples do not turn brown.

In a small bowl add the rest of the lime juice, mustard, oil, honey, and salt. Whisk until well blended. Set aside.

Add the rest of the ingredients to the apples. Toss to combine completely. Add the dressing, and toss again.

Give everyone the benefit of the doubt. Do not judge others by their looks or the size of their bank account.
- Gary Langbaum

BOK CHOY SALAD WITH BLUEBERRY CINNAMON DRESSING

Blueberry Cinnamon Dressing:

2 tbsp. fresh or thawed blueberries	1/8 tsp. lemon juice
	1 tsp. cinnamon
3 tbsp. olive oil	4 tbsp. water

Place all ingredients into a mini food processor or mini blender. Process until a dressing consistency. If too thick, add more water. Set aside.

Salad:

2 stalks of bok choy, including greens, chopped	4 radishes, cut into matchstick shapes
1/2 c. shredded red cabbage	1/4 c. chickpeas
2 stalks green onion, (scallions), chopped	1/2 c. sliced almonds
	1/2 c. fresh or frozen blueberries

Mix all vegetables together in a chilled serving bowl. Blend in the chick peas. Fold in the almonds. Gently fold in the blueberries.

Spoon the Blueberry Cinnamon Dressing over the salad and toss.

Children, refrain from making adult decisions until you are old enough to understand the consequences.
- Teri Paradiso

STRAWBERRY WALNUT SALAD WITH GOAT CHEESE

Toasted Walnuts:

1/2 c. walnuts, chopped

8 c. baby spinach, cleaned

1/4 of a red onion,
  sliced very thin

1/2 cucumber,
  peeled, and diced

1/2 can black olives

1/2 c. strawberries, sliced

4 oz. goat cheese

In a large dry pan on medium-low heat, cook walnuts for 1 to 2 minutes. Move frequently toasting all sides. Set aside.

In a large chilled bowl add all ingredients (except the walnuts, strawberries and goat cheese). Add the dressing and toss.

Gently fold in the walnuts, strawberries and goat cheese.

Strawberry Walnut Dressing:

1/4 c. olive oil

2 tbsp. apple cider vinegar

1/2 tsp. mustard,
  made with apple cider
  vinegar

1/2 c. strawberries

1/4 c. walnuts

Sea salt & pepper to taste

Place all ingredients in a food processor or a high powered blender. Process until smooth.

I can do all things through Him who strengthens me.
~ Philippians - 4:13

Vegetables & Side Dishes

SAUCES

WHITE SAUCE	Liquid	Thickening	Fat	Salt
No.1 thin	1 c. milk	1 tbsp. flour	1 tbsp.	1/2 tsp.
No.2 medium	1 c. milk	2 tbsp. flour	1-1/2 tbsp.	1-1/2 tsp.
No.3	1 c. milk	3 tbsp. flour	2 tbsp.	1 tsp.
No.4 thick	1 c. milk	4 tbsp. flour	2-1/2 tbsp.	1 tsp.

Use No.1 sauce for cream soups. Use No.2 sauce for creamed or scalloped dishes or gravy. Use No.3 sauce for soufflés. Use No.4 sauce for croquettes.

VEGETABLE TIMETABLE - MINUTES

VEGETABLE	Boiled	Steamed	Baked
Asparagus Tips	10-15		
Asparagus, tied in bundles	20-30		
Artichokes, French	40	45-60	
Bean, Lima	20-40	60	
Bean, String	15-35	60	
Beets, young with skins on	30	60	70-90
Beets, old	60-120	60-120	
Broccoli, flowerets	5-10		
Broccoli, stems	20-30		
Brussel Sprouts	20-30		
Cabbage, chopped	10-20	25	
Cauliflower, stem down	20-30		
Cauliflower, flowerets	8-10		
Carrots, cut across	20-30	40	
Chard	60-90	90	
Celery, 1-1/2 inch pieces	20-30	45	
Corn, green, tender	5-10	15	20
Corn on the cob	8-10	15	
Eggplant, whole	30	40	45
Marrow	15-40		
Onions	25-40	60	60
Parsnips	25-40	60	60-75
Peas, green	5-15	5-15	
Peppers	20-30	30	30
Potatoes, depending on size	20-40	60	45-60
Potatoes, sweet	40	40	45-60
Scalloped potatoes			60-90
Pumpkin, in cubes	30	45	60
Tomatoes, depending on size	5-15	50	15-20
Turnips, depending on size	25-40		

CAJUN CARROT FRIES

6 large carrots,
   washed and peeled
1 tbsp. extra-virgin olive oil
1/4 tsp. pepper

1/4 tsp. onion powder
1/4 tsp. garlic powder
1/4 tsp. cayenne pepper
1/4 tsp. paprika

Cut each carrot in half. Cut each half into thin sticks.

In a large bowl place olive oil. Mix in carrots and toss until evenly coated. In a separate, small bowl, combine spices. Dust carrot slices with the spice mix.

Line a baking sheet with parchment paper or silicone mat.

Add carrots lined up in a single layer. Bake at 425 F for 18 to 20 minutes or until carrots are browned and crisp.

NOTE: Halfway through, turn carrots to cook on other side.

ROASTED BRUSSELS SPROUTS

1 lb. fresh Brussels sprouts,
   washed
2 tbsp. olive oil

1/2 tsp. sea salt
1/2 tsp. garlic powder
Ground pepper to taste

Cut off and discard the stem end and any yellow or brown leaves. Cut each sprout in half lengthwise, if choosing this option.

In a large bowl mix sprouts, olive oil, seasoning and toss together.

Put sprouts in a baking pan lined with parchment paper or a silicone mat. Bake at 400 F for 30 minutes or until crispy on outside and tender on the inside.

** Brussels sprouts can also be cooked whole as an option. May need to cook them 5 minutes more. They are great either way.

GREEN BEAN ALMONDINE

2 tbsp. olive oil

1 lb. fresh green beans,
    cleaned & ends cut off

1 large onion, sliced

1/4 c. sliced almonds

Sea salt & pepper to taste

Garlic powder to taste

In a large skillet on medium-high heat, boil water. Add green beans. Boil water again and then lower heat to medium. Partially cover and cook for 5 minutes. Drain. Rinse and dry skillet.

In same large skillet heat olive oil on medium heat. Add onions and cook until slightly browned. Add green beans, almonds, and seasonings. Mix everything together and cook for 5 minutes. Almonds should be golden brown and green beans crisp.

ROASTED ASPARAGUS WITH LEMON DRIZZLE

1 bunch asparagus

2 tbsp. olive oil

1/2 tsp. garlic powder

1/2 tsp. sea salt

Lemon juice
    from 1/2 fresh lemon

Wash and trim dried parts from bottom of asparagus stalks, removing 1/2 inch.

In a shallow baking dish, line asparagus spears side by side. Drizzle with oil and sprinkle with salt and garlic. Roll them a bit and repeat until all sides are coated.

Roast in oven at 350 F for 10 to12 minutes or until tips slightly brown. Place in serving platter and drizzle with fresh lemon.

The healthy way to be in control is to be secure enough in yourself, that outside events do not threaten your coping skills.
- Deepak Chopra

KALE WITH GARLIC AND OIL

1 bunch of kale, leaves pulled
    from ribs & cut
3 tbsp. olive oil

4 garlic cloves, chopped
1/2 tsp. garlic powder
1/2 tsp. sea salt

Boil 1 cup water in large pot. Add kale and cook for 5 minutes. Drain and let dry.

Heat oil in a large skillet over medium heat. Add garlic and sauté for 3 minutes. Add kale to the garlic and oil. Season with garlic powder and salt. Toss and sauté for another 3 minutes.

SEASONED ROASTED BEETS

4 medium beets
3 tbsp. olive oil
1/2 tsp. sea salt

1/2 tsp. fresh cracked pepper
1 large onion, finely chopped
3 garlic cloves, minced

Wash beets, scrubbing well, to remove all dirt. Cut each beet into 6 wedges. Place beets in a 9 x 13 inch baking dish. Drizzle with half the oil. Season with salt, and pepper. Cover dish. Roast at 375 F for one hour. Turn beets and cook uncovered, for 15 more minutes, or until desired tenderness.

Place beets in a serving bowl. Add the onion, garlic and the rest of the oil. Toss and serve.

GARLIC ROASTED BROCCOLI FLORETS

1 lb. broccoli florets, cleaned
1 tbsp. extra-virgin olive oil

2 garlic cloves, minced
Salt and pepper to taste

In a large bowl, toss broccoli with olive oil. Add garlic, salt and pepper and toss again. Place broccoli in a baking dish and roast at 400 F for 30 minutes or until browned.

NOTE: Halfway through, turn to cook the other side.

CAULIFLOWER MASHED

1 large head cauliflower
1/2 stick of butter
1/4 c. grated cheese
  (optional)

Salt & pepper to taste
1/2 tsp. garlic powder

Clean and cut cauliflower into small pieces.

Boil 2 cups salted water. Add cauliflower and cook on medium-high heat for about 10 minutes or until very tender. Drain and add butter and seasonings.

Mash cauliflower with potato masher to desired texture.

To cut down on odors from cauliflower, add 1 teaspoon vinegar to water.

BOK CHOY STIR-FRY WITH GARLIC AND GINGER

1 tbsp. coconut oil
3 cloves garlic, chopped
1 in. fresh ginger,
  peeled and chopped

1 bunch bok choy
2 tbsp. coconut aminos
1/4 tsp. sea salt
Ground pepper to taste

Wash bok choy, trim ends to discard and cut into 1/2 inch pieces. Chop the greens.

Heat oil in large skillet over medium heat. Add garlic and ginger and cook 1 minute or until slightly browned.

Add bok choy and aminos. Cook for 4 minutes or until greens are wilted and stalks are crisp, yet tender. Season with salt and pepper.

Be a light, not a judge, be a model, not a critic.
- Stephen Covey

BAKED TWICE ACORN SQUASH

1 medium to large size acorn squash, uncooked	1/2 tsp. paprika, for filling
4 scallions, chopped	2 tbsp. almond flour
1/2 c. cream cheese	2 tbsp. grated Parmesan, for topping
Salt, to taste	1/2 tsp. paprika, for topping

Wash and cut acorn squash crosswise. Cut off ends on each side, just enough to sit flat, but not pierce skin. Remove seeds.

Place in shallow baking dish, cut side up. Add 1/4 cup water. Bake at 400 F for 40 minutes or until tender. Allow to cool enough to handle.

Remove the meat of the squash with a spoon, and into a large bowl, leaving a 1/4 inch border to keep its shape. Be careful not to pierce or break skin.

Add to the squash bowl, scallions, cream cheese, salt, and paprika. Mash together with a hand masher or electric mixer until well blended and smooth. Fill squash stuffing into shells.

In a small, dry skillet, on medium heat, toast almond flour. Move skillet back and forth and cook for 2 minutes, until browned.

In a small bowl, mix together almond flour, Parmesan, and paprika. Sprinkle almond mix on top of filling. Bake at 400 F for 20 minutes or until golden brown.

This recipe can also be made using a small butternut squash. You can also use Greek yogurt or sour cream instead of the cream cheese.

When we are truly strong in the hard moments, everything else is essentially, "cake".
- Stephen R. Covey

GREEN BEAN CASSEROLE WITH CRISPY ONION RINGS

Fried Onion Rings:

1 c. milk

1 egg, beaten

3 medium onions,
    sliced into thin rings

2 c. almond flour

1/3 c. arrowroot flour

1 tsp. sea salt

1/2 tsp. paprika

1/2 tsp. chili powder or
    cayenne pepper

1/4 tsp. black pepper

1/3 c. grapeseed oil

In a large bowl, whisk the milk into the beaten egg. Place the arrowroot flour in a shallow dish. Place the almond flour and spices in a separate shallow dish, and combine.

Meanwhile, heat oil over medium high heat.

Separate the onion rings. Place the rings, a few at a time, into the egg mixture, and coat well.

Using a fork, place rings, one at a time, into the arrowroot flour, and coat well. Put the onion back into the egg mixture to coat again. Finally, place the onion into the almond flour mixture. Coat thoroughly.

When oil is hot, place onions into oil and fry until crispy and golden brown. Set aside and place on paper towel, to soak up oil.

Green Bean Casserole:

2 lb. fresh green beans,
    clean and cut into
    2 in. pieces

1/2 c. Greek yogurt

1 large onion, sliced thin

2 tbsp. olive oil

2 tsp. coconut aminos

In a pot of boiling water, cook green beans for 5 minutes or until al dente. Drain beans and rinse in cool water so they don't continue to cook. Place in a large bowl and set aside.

In a large skillet, heat oil over medium heat. Add onions and cook, until they are slightly brown. Remove from heat. Set aside.

Continued...

In a large bowl, add yogurt and aminos and mix well. Add green beans, onions, and combine.

Mix onion rings into green bean mixture. Can save some onion rings to put on top. Place green bean mixture into a greased casserole dish. Cover dish. Bake at 350 F for 20 minutes or until heated through.

** Onion rings also make a great appetizer, snack, or complement to steaks or burgers.

CHINESE VEGETABLE FRIED QUINOA

1/4 c. olive oil (4 tbsp.)

1 large yellow onion, chopped

1 c. scallions, (green onions) diagonally chopped

3 c. cooked quinoa, cold from refrigerator

2 eggs, beaten

3 tbsp. coconut aminos

1/4 tsp. sea salt

1 c. chopped bok choy, or celery

1 c. peas, frozen, thawed

3/4 c. carrots, chopped

Heat skillet on medium heat. Add 2 tablespoons of olive oil. (Use the other 2 tablespoons of oil as needed.) Cook onions and scallions until lightly browned. Add quinoa and sauté until lightly crispy.

In a small bowl, beat together, eggs, aminos and salt. Pour over quinoa mixture and wait about 30 seconds allowing the eggs to cook slightly from the heat. Eggs will form small pieces of scrambled egg. Stir to combine. Add vegetables and cook about 8 minutes or until done.

Choose not to complain, instead...be the change you want to see.
- Teri Paradiso

MAC AND CHEESE

16 oz. quinoa pasta
3 c. 2% or whole milk
1 tsp. arrowroot flour
1/4 tsp. sea salt
2 tbsp. butter

2 tbsp. cream cheese
1/2 tsp. paprika
1/2 tsp. garlic powder
3 c. grated mild Cheddar
cheese

Bring a large pot of water to a boil. Add the pasta and cook for 3 minutes less than the package instructions suggest. Drain.

Meanwhile, make the sauce. Combine the milk, arrowroot flour, and salt in a medium bowl and whisk to combine.

Place the butter and cream cheese in a large pot and heat over medium heat. When cream cheese is soft and butter has melted, slowly whisk in the milk mixture. Cook, stirring, until the mixture is hot and has thickened slightly, about 3 minutes. Add the paprika, and garlic powder. Reduce heat to low and add the cheese. Cook, stirring frequently, until thickened.

Add the pasta to the sauce. Stir and cook for about 1 minute, to combine the pasta and sauce.

** NOTE: Quinoa pasta is made with either corn or rice which are both grains. If you choose to use quinoa pasta buy the rice. The corn, may be genetically modified and contaminated.

RICE WITHOUT THE GRAIN

2 tbsp. olive oil
1 large onion, chopped
2 garlic cloves, chopped
1 fresh roasted red pepper,
    finely chopped

2 c. quinoa,
    cooked according to
    directions
Salt & pepper to taste
1 tbsp. fresh parsley, chopped

Heat olive oil in a large skillet on medium heat. Add and sauté onions and red pepper. When onions are translucent and pepper tender, add garlic and cook for another minute. Add cooked quinoa, and seasonings. Combine. Lower heat to simmer, cover and cook until quinoa is heated, slightly browned and crispy.

SPAGHETTI SQUASH
WITH CARROTS AND SCALLIONS

1 small spaghetti squash
4 large carrots,
**   peeled, cut julienne style**
3 tbsp. coconut oil

7 scallions (green onions),
**   sliced**
Salt to taste
Cayenne pepper to taste

Wash spaghetti squash. No need to cut. Cook in oven in shallow dish at 400 F for 45 minutes. It will be hot, so hold squash with oven mitt or paper towel.

Cut squash lengthwise. Hold one end with hand, and with a fork, take the seeds and pulp out. Can throw out or save and bake like you would pumpkin seeds in oven.

Holding squash upright in a large bowl, scrape the squash with the fork, from top to bottom, bringing the squash into the bowl. Continue this with both halves. Cover to keep warm.

Heat coconut oil in pan over medium-high heat. Add carrots and sauté until slightly browned.

Put scallions in pot with carrots and sauté for 2 minutes.

Add squash and mix together. Lower to simmer and cook for 4 minutes. Season with salt and cayenne pepper to taste.

** This is a sweet side dish that can complement most meals.

Habits don't always need to be unhealthy. Healthy habits have long lasting benefits.
- Teri Paradiso

WALNUT RAISIN STUFFING

2 tbsp. coconut oil
1 small onion, chopped
3 stalks celery, chopped
1/4 c. raisins
1/4 c. walnuts, chopped
3/4 c. sesame butter
3 eggs

1/2 tsp. sea salt
1/4 tsp. pepper
2 tsp. sage
1/4 tsp. powdered dried thyme
1/2 c. quinoa, cooked according to directions

Heat coconut oil in skillet. Add onions, celery, raisins and walnuts. Cook until tender. Remove from heat and reserve.

Place sesame butter, eggs, salt, pepper and herbs into a food processor or high powered blender. Process until smooth.

Pour sesame mixture into a large mixing bowl. Add the walnut and raisin mixture. Add the quinoa. Combine until everything is evenly mixed.

Pour mixture into a greased 9x9 inch baking dish. Bake at 350 F for 45 minutes. When inserted toothpick comes out clean it will be done.

** This is a great complement to turkey and chicken dinners.
Tip: For a change use chopped apples instead of raisins.

Your word is a lamp that gives light wherever I walk.
- Psalms 119:105

Main Dishes

SPICE GUIDE

Keep spices in tightly covered containers, in a cool dry place. After about a year, spices tend to lose flavor so more may be needed for seasonings. Overheating can cause spices to turn bitter. During lengthy cooking, add spices during the last half hour of cooking time. Usually 1 teaspoon of dried herb equals 1 tablespoon of fresh.

ALLSPICE: *Flavor a blend of cinnamon, cloves and nutmeg.* Meat dishes, egg dishes, fish, gravies, pickles, relishes, tomato sauce, fruit preserves.

BASIL: *Pungent, sweet aroma.* Broiled and roasted meats and poultry, fish, egg dishes, soups, vegetables, tomato dishes, pasta, dressings, sauces.

BAY LEAF: *Strong flavor.* Stews, soups, vegetables, pickles, gravies, sauces, marinades.

CAYENNE: *Red pepper, very hot.* Meats, seafoods, egg and cheese dishes, soups, sauces, dips, spreads, French dressing.

CHILI POWDER: *Hot, peppery blend of herbs and spices.* Spanish or Mexican dishes, bean and rice dishes, barbeque and cocktail sauces, spreads, dressings, dips, egg dishes, vegetables.

CINNAMON: *Sweet, spicy aroma.* Breads, cookies, cakes, desserts, pastries, beverages, sauces, vegetables.

CLOVES: *Strong, spicy-sweet aroma.* Pork and lamb dishes, barbeque sauce, pickles, relishes, fruits, breads, cakes, cookies, desserts.

CUMIN: *Strong, slightly bitter, lemon flavor.* Spanish, Mexican and Eastern dishes, stews, pickles, tomato dishes.

CURRY: *A blend of many spices; warm and sharp to hot and spicy.* Meat, seafood, egg and cheese dishes, soups, sauces, seafood, salads, dips.

DILL SEED: *Mild, slight caraway-like flavor.* Meats, poultry, fish, seafood, stews, soups, salads, sauces, dressings, dips, pickles, breads, egg dishes.

GINGER: *Pleasant odor, pungent taste.* Oriental dishes, meats, vegetables, fruits, salad dressings, pickles, jams, marinades, breads, desserts.

MARJORAM: *Spicy, sweet aroma.* Roasted meats and poultry, fish and seafood, egg dishes, stews and casseroles, soups, vegetables, salads, gravies.

MUSTARD: *Pungent taste.* Pickles, relishes, salad dressings, sauces, dips, egg dishes, marinades, pork and ham, corned beef.

NUTMEG: *Warm, sweet, spicy flavor.* Vegetables, egg dishes, beverages, breads, cookies, cakes, desserts, sauces.

OREGANO: *Strong and aromatic.* Italian dishes, pizza and pasta, broiled and roasted meats, fish and seafood, stews and casseroles, egg dishes, tomato sauces, soups, vegetables, salads, salad dressings.

PAPRIKA: *Varies from mild, slightly sweet to hot; adds colour to many dishes.* Meats, poultry, salad dressings, dips, vegetables, soups and salads.

PARSLEY: *Mild flavor.* Brings out the flavor of most non-sweet foods.

ROSEMARY: *Sweet, spicy, pine-like fragrance.* Roasted meat and poultry, fish, stews, casseroles, stuffings, salads, breads, egg dishes.

SAGE: *Strong, slightly bitter.* Roasted meats and poultry, fish, stuffings, vegetables, cheese dishes, salads, gravies, sauces.

MAMA TRAMONTANO'S
ITALIAN MEATLOAF WITH RAISINS

2 lb. ground beef
3/4 c. flax seed meal, reserve
   1/4 for dusting
1 tbsp. garlic powder
1/4 c. fresh basil
1/4 c. fresh parsley
1/2 tsp. sea salt
1/2 tsp. black pepper
1/2 tsp. cayenne pepper

2 eggs, beaten
1/2 c. grated cheese
1 1/2 c. raisins, soaked in
   water just to plump up
3 tbsp. olive oil
1 large onion, chopped
1 28 oz. crushed tomatoes
1/4 can water from the
   crushed tomato can

In a large bowl, with clean hands or gloves, mix meat, flax seed meal, all the seasonings, eggs, and grated cheese.

Separate mixture into 3 or 4 even sections, and form each into a ball.

Sprinkle a little flax meal on parchment paper so meat does not stick. Put one ball of meat mixture on parchment paper. Flatten out with your hands, forming a large circle. Cover the circle evenly with raisins.

Roll the meat and raisins up like a jelly roll, to form a long loaf. Be sure it will fit in skillet. Wet your hands and press sides and ends to seal. Repeat with other sections.

In a large skillet, heat oil on medium high heat, and sauté onions until lightly browned. Add the meatloaf, and cook on all sides, until golden brown and crisp.

Pour sauce and water over the meatloaf and cook for another 5 minutes at this temperature.

Adjust the temperature to medium-low. Cook for 1 hour, occasionally turning and basting meat with the sauce.

** For a great idea, mama Tramontano puts peas in the same skillet, towards the end of cooking, and cooks them in the sauce.

QUINOA PASTA & MEATBALLS

Meatballs:

3 lb. ground beef

1/2 c. almond flour

2 tbsp. garlic powder

1/4 c. fresh basil or
2 tbsp. dried

1/4 c. fresh parsley or
2 tbsp. dried

1 tsp. sea salt

1/2 tsp. black pepper

1/4 tsp. cayenne pepper

2 large eggs, beaten

3/4 c. grated cheese

3 tbsp. extra virgin olive oil

1 large onion, chopped

In a large mixing bowl, add meat, almond flour, all the seasonings, eggs and grated cheese. Mix with gloves or clean hands until thoroughly combined. Form the mixture into 3 inch meatballs.

Heat oil in large pot on medium heat. Pot should be large enough to add the sauce to it. Add onions and sauté until translucent. Add meatballs. Fry meatballs and turn until all sides are browned.

Sauce:

2 28 oz. can crushed tomatoes
& 1/2 can of water

2 tsp. garlic powder

2 tbsp. of fresh parsley
or 1 tsp. dried

2 tbsp. of fresh basil
or 1 tsp. dried

1 tsp. dried oregano

1 tsp. black pepper

1/2 tsp. cayenne pepper

1 tsp. sea salt

In same pot as meatballs and onions, add in crushed tomatoes, plus ½ can of water, and all the seasonings.

Stir gently with a wooden spoon being careful not to break up the meatballs. Continue to cook on medium heat, with the pot covered 3/4 of the way. Continue to check and stir periodically. Cook for at least 3 hours. The longer it cooks, the better it tastes.

Continued...

Quinoa Pasta:
3 8 oz. boxes of quinoa fusilli   **2 tbsp. grated cheese**
    pasta

Cook pasta according to directions. I like my pasta al dente which just means firm. The instructions say 13 to 15 minutes but test the pasta at 10 minutes and cook to your liking. Drain pasta.

Add a little sauce to the serving platter. Add some pasta and more sauce, mixing gently as you go. You can top off with a little grated cheese. Gently remove meatballs from pot and onto another serving platter. Serve immediately.

** NOTE: Quinoa pasta is made with a little corn or rice flour in the ingredients. If you choose to make it, choose the brand Andean Dream. They make it with a little rice flour, and no corn.

POT ROAST

2 tbsp. olive oil   **2 bay leaves**

5 lb. beef chuck roast   **2 sprigs of thyme**

Salt and pepper to taste   **2 lb. celery,**
2 c. beef stock, yeast free   **cut into 1 1/2 in. slices**

3 cloves garlic, chopped   **2 lb. carrots,**
3 large onions, cut into chunks   **cut into 1 1/2 in. slices**

3 tbsp. tomato paste   **1 16 oz. bag frozen peas**

In a large Dutch oven, heat olive oil over medium-high heat. Season roast with salt and pepper all over. Brown roast thoroughly on all sides for about 10 minutes.

Add stock, garlic, onions, tomatoes, bay leaves and thyme. Bring to a simmer. Cover and put in oven on 350 F and cook for 3 hours. Add the celery and carrots. Cook for 45 minutes more. Add peas and cook for another 15 minutes.

PAN-SEARED RIB-EYE STEAKS

2 tbsp. honey
2 tbsp. mustard
2 tbsp. juice from fresh lemon
2 rib-eye steaks,
    about 8 oz. each

2 tbsp. olive oil
Sea salt to taste
Freshly ground black pepper
    to taste

In a small bowl, whisk together honey, mustard and lemon juice. Set aside. Pat steaks dry. Coat with olive oil. Season steaks with salt and pepper.

On high heat, in a large skillet, heat the rest of the olive oil. When oil begins to smoke, add steaks. Cook steaks for 2 to 3 minutes on one side, to create a sear. When steaks are browned, use a tong to flip the steaks over. Sear the other side for 2 to 3 minutes. This should result in a medium-rare steak. Alter your cooking time for your desired preference. Brush honey mixture over steaks.

BAKED CHICKEN FINGERS

2 c. whole almonds
1 tsp. garlic powder
2 tsp. paprika
1 tsp. dry mustard
1/4 tsp. cayenne pepper

1/4 tsp. sea salt
2 eggs, beaten
1 1/2 lb. chicken strips
1 tbsp. grape seed oil

Place almonds in a large zip-lock bag. Using a meat mallet, crush almonds until the size of coarse bread crumbs. Add seasonings to the bag. Shake to mix. Pour almond mixture into a shallow plate. Whisk eggs in a shallow bowl. One at a time, using a fork, add chicken strips to eggs and coat both sides evenly. Place the chicken into the almond mixture, again, coat both sides evenly.

Line a baking sheet with parchment paper or silicone mat. Place chicken fingers side by side. Drizzle or spray grapeseed oil over the chicken fingers. Bake at 475 F for 20 to 25 minutes or until chicken fingers are cooked through, golden brown and crispy. Turn halfway through cooking.

PARMIGIANO CHICKEN

4 chicken breasts, boneless
and skinless
2 c. almond flour
Salt and pepper to taste
2 eggs, beaten
4 tbsp. olive oil
2 c. crushed tomatoes

1/2 c. water
5 garlic cloves, chopped
2 tbsp. fresh basil leaves,
chopped
16 oz. fresh mozzarella
cheese, sliced

Slice chicken breasts horizontally, to make them thinner. Pat dry.

Mix almond flour, salt and pepper in a platter. Using a fork, place cutlets in the eggs, and coat well. Place the cutlets into the almond flour, coating both sides.

In a large skillet, heat oil over medium heat. Add cutlets and sauté until golden brown, about 5 minutes on each side.

Remove cutlets from skillet. Set aside.

In same pan, add crushed tomatoes, water, garlic, and basil. Simmer for 15 minutes.

In a 9 x 16 inch baking dish, add 1/2 cup of sauce.

Place cutlets in the dish in a single layer. Add the rest of the sauce. Cover the cutlets and sauce with the mozzarella cheese.

Bake at 365 F for 15 minutes.

*Identify your problems but give your power and energy
to solutions.
- Tony Robbins*

SOFT CHICKEN TORTILLAS

Tortilla:

2 c. quinoa flour

2 tbsp. olive oil

1 tsp. sea salt

2/3 c. hot water

1/2 c. quinoa flour to help form the dough ball

In a medium size bowl mix flour, 1 tablespoon of oil and salt. Pour in the hot water, adding a little extra if needed, and combine to form a dough. With gloves or clean hands, knead dough for 2 minutes. Add the other tbsp. of oil, pouring it over the dough. Cover bowl and let sit for 15 minutes.

Put the quinoa flour on a board or other clean, flat surface. Put some flour on your hands, because the dough is sticky. Take a golf size ball amount of dough and roll it into the quinoa flour on the board, forming the ball.

Put the dough between two small squares of parchment paper and place in your tortilla press. I sprinkle some flour on the bottom piece of parchment paper. Be careful to only press gently.

Heat dry skillet on high. Lift top parchment paper off and turn tortilla over. Place in dry skillet. The other piece of parchment paper will now be on top. Holding the paper up off the skillet, let the tortilla cook in skillet up to 60 seconds or until you can gently lift the paper off the tortilla. Cook for a few more seconds, until you see little bubbles. Turn and cook for 1 minute on other side, or until just lightly browned. Set aside. Place in dish and continue until all tortillas are cooked.

Chicken Fajitas:

2 tbsp. olive oil

1 c. boneless chicken, cooked & shred

3 c. red, orange, and yellow bell peppers

1 large onion, sliced thin

1/2 tsp. garlic powder

1/2 tsp. chili powder

1/2 tsp. curry powder

1/4 tsp. cayenne powder

1/4 c. salsa,

1/2 c. shredded Cheddar cheese (optional)

1/4 c. sour cream

Continued...

In a large skillet, heat oil on medium heat. Sauté the peppers and onions until onions are translucent, about 4 minutes. Add the chicken, garlic, curry, chili and cayenne. Mix and allow to cook, stirring frequently. Cook for 7 to 10 minutes or until chicken is heated through.

Add a little sour cream to tortilla, then the chicken mixture, cheese (optional), and the salsa.

** You will love these no grain soft tortillas.

CHICKEN CACCIATORE

6 chicken breasts cleaned, with skin and bone

3 tbsp. olive oil

1 large onion, chopped

3 garlic cloves, finely chopped

1 28 oz. can crushed tomatoes

1/3 of the tomato can filled with water

1/2 c. organic gluten free vegetable broth

4 tbsp. drained capers

2 tsp. dried oregano

1/4 tsp. sea salt

1 tsp. freshly ground black pepper

1/4 c. fresh basil leaves, chopped

In a large, heavy sauté pan, heat oil on medium-high heat. Add the chicken breasts and sauté until brown, about 5 minutes each side. Transfer the chicken to a plate and set aside.

To the same pan, add the onion and garlic, and sauté until onion is translucent, about 5 minutes. Add tomatoes, water, broth, capers, oregano, salt, pepper and basil. Cook for 5 minutes.

Return the chicken breasts to the pan. Spoon the sauce over the chicken. Lower the heat to medium-low, cover and cook for 30 minutes or until well cooked through. Halfway through, turn chicken and spoon sauce over the chicken again.

OVEN ROASTED TURKEY WITH BROWN GRAVY

Oven Roasted Turkey:

12 lb. turkey, cleaned, and insides removed

1 1/2 sticks butter, at room temperature

1 tsp. sea salt

1 tsp. freshly ground pepper

Butter the whole turkey inside and out, on all sides. Sprinkle turkey with salt and pepper. Turn turkey to breast side down, so juice goes into the breast meat.

Put turkey into a brown paper bag, or cut the bag, and make a tent to cover the top of the turkey. This will keep the turkey from burning or drying out.

Put turkey on bottom rack in oven. Cook at 350 F. Cooking time is 15 minutes for each pound of turkey. To test if turkey is done the thermometer should read 160 degrees for white meat and 170 degrees for dark meat. The temperature will continue to rise when you take the turkey out of the oven and will end up at 165 F for white meat and 175 F for dark meat. Let turkey rest for at least 30 minutes before carving.

Carve the turkey with a slicing knife against the grain. Slice turkey as thin as possible. The thinner the slice, the shorter the muscle strands, and the more tender the turkey will be.

Brown Gravy:

Pan drippings from turkey

1 tbsp. arrowroot powder

1 c. warm water

Sea salt to taste

Pour the pan drippings through a fine-mesh sieve, or through a fine-mesh strainer, into a medium size pan. The mesh will catch any turkey pieces.

Heat the drippings on medium low-heat. Add 1 tablespoon arrowroot powder to a cup of warm water, and mix until there are no lumps. When the juice heats to a low boil, slowly pour the arrowroot into the juice. Stir continuously until the gravy begins to thicken.

Continued...

If gravy does not thicken, add more arrowroot and water to adjust to the thickness you want. Add salt.

Arrowroot is best used just at the end of cooking the juice, because continued heating will cause it to lose its thickening ability. Keep warm until serving. I have a gravy server that keeps the gravy hot for a couple hours.

PAN-SEARED SALMON WITH STRAWBERRY SALSA

Strawberry Salsa:

1 c. organic strawberries, finely diced

2 green onions (scallions) thinly sliced

1/4 of an avocado, finely diced

1 tbsp. jalapeños, finely diced

1/2 tsp. fresh lime juice

1 tbsp. cilantro, finely chopped

Sea salt and pepper to taste

2 tsp. olive oil

In a medium size bowl, combine all ingredients and mix well. Set aside.

Salmon Fillets:

4 skinless salmon fillets

2 tbsp. coconut oil

Sea salt and pepper to taste

Clean and pat dry salmon fillets with paper towels.

In a large skillet, heat coconut oil over medium-high heat. Place salmon in skillet and season with salt and pepper. Pan-fry salmon for 4 to 6 minutes on each side, or until nicely browned. Time cooked will depend on thickness of salmon.

Place on serving plate and top with strawberry salsa.

ALMOND CRUSTED SALMON

1/4 c. whole almonds
1 tsp. garlic powder
1 tsp. chili powder
1 tsp. paprika

1/4 tsp. black pepper
3 tbsp. olive oil
2 Sockeye salmon fillets,
  thawed

Place almonds in a large zip-lock bag. Using a meat mallet, crush almonds until the size of coarse bread crumbs. Add seasonings to the bag with almonds. Shake to mix.

Coat salmon with 1 tablespoon olive oil and then place salmon in the zip-lock bag. Shake bag and press salmon with fingertips to evenly coat.

In a large skillet, heat 2 tablespoons olive oil on medium heat. Add salmon and cook 4 to 5 minutes each side. Time will also depend on thickness of salmon.

SNAPPER ALMONDINE

3/4 c. almond flour
Salt & pepper to taste
4 8 oz. snapper fillets,
  cleaned and patted dry
4 tsp. grapeseed oil
  for brushing

1/4 c. grapeseed oil
1/4 c. butter
1 tbsp. juice from fresh lemon
1/2 c. sliced almonds
2 tbsp. chopped parsley, fresh

Place almond flour in a shallow dish. Add salt and pepper and combine. Brush fillets with oil on both sides and then coat with almond flour.

Heat butter and oil on medium-high heat. Sauté fillets for about 4 to 5 minutes on each side, according to the thickness of the fillets. Remove to a heated dish. Add lemon juice, almonds and parsley to remaining butter and oil. Sauté until almonds are golden brown. Pour sauce over fillets.

** I like to make this dish with cauliflower mashed and kale sautéed in garlic and oil. Delish!

FLOUNDER IN LEMON BUTTER SAUCE

1/4 c. almond flour	4 tbsp. butter
1/8 tsp. sea salt	2 garlic cloves, minced
1 tsp. dried parsley,	Juice of 1 lemon
to mix in flour	1/4 c. fresh parsley,
1 tbsp. olive oil	coarsely chopped
2 fillets of flounder	

Place almond flour in a flat platter. Add salt and dried parsley and combine. Brush fillets with olive oil on both sides.

Using a fork, place fillets, one at a time, in the almond flour and coat both sides completely.

Heat 1 tablespoon of butter in a large skillet over medium heat.

Add fillets and cook for 3 minutes on the one side. Add another tablespoon of butter in skillet. Turn the flounder over to cook the other side. Cook for 3 minutes or until it separates easily with a fork. Remove from pan and keep warm.

In the same pan, place 2 tablespoons butter and garlic. Sauté garlic for two minutes. Add the lemon juice, stir and cook for another minute. Stir in parsley. Remove from heat. Spoon sauce over the fillets.

You will see it when you believe it.
- Wayne W. Dyer

GRILLED SALMON
WITH MANGO SALSA

Grilled Salmon:

6 salmon fillets, skinless	Sea salt and pepper to taste
1 tbsp. olive oil	6 lime wedges for garnish

Coat salmon fillets with olive oil. Sprinkle with salt and pepper. Place fillets on grill. Meanwhile, prepare the mango salsa. Grill the salmon for 5 to 7 minutes on each side, or until cooked through and done to your preference.

Drape the salsa over the salmon fillets and garnish with a wedge.

Mango Salsa:

1 1/2 c. fresh mango, peeled, pitted and diced	1 tbsp. jalapeño, finely diced
	juice from 1 fresh lime
2 tbsp. red bell pepper, finely diced	1 tsp. curry powder
	salt to taste
2 tbsp. red onion, finely diced	

In a medium bowl, combine all ingredients. Set aside.

Every man should eat and indeed drink, and see good for all his hard work. It is the gift of God.
- Ecclesiastics 3:13

VEGETARIAN BUTTERNUT STEW

1/4 c. olive oil or 4 tbsp.

4 onions, sliced

1 large butternut squash, peeled & cut into 1 in. cubes

5 garlic cloves, minced

4 medium red bell peppers, sliced, julienne

4 sage leaves or 1 tbsp. dried

1 c. water

1 bunch kale, pull leaves from ribs & chop

3 15 oz. white cannellini beans, with juice

Salt and pepper , to taste

Grated Parmesan cheese (optional)

Heat oil on medium heat in a large pot. Add onions, and sauté until translucent. Add squash, peppers, garlic, and sage. Cover pot, lower to simmer and sauté for 10 minutes. Add water and continue to cook for another 8 minutes or until tender.

Mix in, kale, beans (with juice), salt and pepper. Cover and simmer until kale is tender. Transfer to serving bowl. Top with Parmesan if you choose.

VEGETABLE FRITTATA

6 eggs

1/3 c. feta cheese

2 tbsp. olive oil

1 onion, chopped

1 yellow bell pepper, chopped

1 red bell pepper, chopped

2 c. spinach, chopped

1/2 tsp. cayenne pepper

1/4 tsp. salt

1/2 tsp. garlic powder

In a large bowl, scramble eggs. Gently fold in the feta cheese.

In an oven proof sauté pan, heat oil on stove top, over medium heat. Add onions and sauté until translucent. Mix in peppers and spices. Cook for another 3 minutes. Add spinach and toss into mixture. Pour the eggs evenly, over mixture, without mixing in. Cook for about 5 minutes. Transfer the oven proof sauté pan into the oven. Bake at 350 F for 7 minutes or until eggs are set, cooked through and golden brown. Cut into wedges.

** This dish is great served with a salad.

TERI'S SPECIAL MARGHERITA PIZZA

Pizza Dough:

1 1/2 c. almond flour	3 eggs
3/4 c. tapioca flour	1/3 c. plain yogurt,
1/3 c. chia seeds	preferably full or low fat
1 tsp. xylitol	Sprinkle oregano, garlic, basil,
1/2 tsp. baking soda	onion, parsley
1/2 tsp. sea salt	

In a large bowl, combine almond flour, tapioca, chia, xylitol, baking soda and salt.

In a smaller bowl, blend eggs and yogurt with an electric mixer just until mixed. Add the egg mixture into the dry ingredients. Use mixer to combine, until it forms a sticky, wet dough.

Pour batter onto a 12x16 inch cookie sheet or 16 inch round pizza pan, lined with parchment paper or a silicone mat. Smooth batter with a spatula, making it thin and even. You can make the dough a little thicker around the sides to form the crust. Sprinkle herbs over dough. Bake at 350 F for 8 minutes, or until tooth-pick comes out clean. NOTE: Do not over bake, or it will be dry.

Pizza sauce:

1 small onion, finely chopped	5 fresh basil leaves, chopped
2 cloves garlic, finely chopped	Sprinkle sea salt, pepper, and
2 tbsp. olive oil	garlic powder
1 14 oz. can tomato sauce	

Heat olive oil in saucepan. Sauté onion and garlic for 1 minute. Add tomato sauce and bring to a gentle boil. Lower heat. Add fresh basil and spices. Simmer for 15 to 20 minutes uncovered.

Pizza Toppings:

2 fresh small tomatoes, round thin slices, or chopped	2 tbsp. olive oil
2 clove garlic, finely chopped	1 tsp. fresh or dried parsley
1 c. fresh mozzarella, sliced round and thin	1 tsp. fresh or dried oregano
10 leaves of fresh basil, chopped	Salt and pepper to taste

Continued...

Brush pizza dough with half the olive oil. Spoon some tomato sauce over dough leaving 1/2 inch for the crust. Evenly distribute the tomatoes, mozzarella, spices and herbs. Drizzle remaining olive oil over pizza. Reserve unused sauce to serve with pizza.

Bake at 425 F for 15 to 20 minutes, or until crisp and golden brown.

** Urban legend holds that the Margherita pizza was named in honor of Queen Margherita in the 1800's. It represents the colors of the Italian flag. the Tomatoes; (red), basil; (green), mozzerella; (white).

MAMA TRAMONTANO'S PASTA PISELLI

4 tbsp. olive oil
3 large onions, chopped
16 oz. peas, frozen
1/2 tsp. sea salt
1/2 tsp. garlic

1/2 tsp. black pepper
2 8 oz. boxes fusilli quinoa pasta, uncooked
1 tbsp. grated cheese (optional)

Heat olive oil in skillet on medium heat. Add onions and sauté until onions are translucent.

In a medium size pot bring 1/2 cup of water to a boil. Add peas, cover and simmer for 4 minutes. Drain. Add peas to the onions and add seasonings. Simmer for another 4 minutes

Cook pasta according to directions. Package says 13 to 15 minutes but check after 10 minutes if you like it al dente (firm). Drain.

Place the pasta in a large serving platter. Spoon the onions and peas over the pasta. Combine evenly. Sprinkle with grated cheese if you desire.

** NOTE: Quinoa pasta is made with rice or corn. If you choose to make it, buy it with the rice flour because corn may be genetically modified.

CRISPY VEGETABLE FAJITAS

Tortillas:

1 c. almond flour	1/2 tsp. sea salt
1/8 c. flax seed meal	1/2 tsp. fresh ground pepper
1/8 c. boiling water	1 tbsp. olive oil

In a medium bowl, combine almond flour, flax seed meal, boiling water, salt, pepper and olive oil. Mix well. Divide dough into 4 equal size parts. Form each into a ball.

Use a tortilla press if you have one. It will make the dough even and thin. Put parchment paper on top and bottom of the dough in the press. Be careful to press only gently. You will still need to put in skillet to cook. If you do not have a press, just follow these directions.

Place each ball in between 2 pieces of parchment paper. Use a rolling pin to roll dough into a 6 inch circle.

Heat a dry skillet on medium-high heat. Take top parchment paper off tortilla, and flip tortilla over and place in skillet. Gently remove the bottom parchment paper. Cook for 2 to 3 minutes on each side, or until golden brown. Repeat with each tortilla. Place each tortilla in a separate dish. Cut into triangles. Set aside

Vegetable Fajitas:

2 tbsp. olive oil	1/2 tsp. chili powder
1 red bell pepper, chopped	1/4 tsp. cayenne pepper
1 green bell pepper, chopped	1/4 c. salsa
1 onion, chopped	1/2 c. shredded Cheddar cheese
1/2 tsp. garlic powder	
1/2 tsp. curry powder	1/4 c. sour cream

In a large skillet, heat olive oil on medium heat. Add and sauté the bell peppers and onions until onions are translucent. Add the garlic, curry, chili and cayenne. Mix and allow to cook, stirring frequently. Cook for 5 to 7 minutes or until peppers and onions are soft. Place 1/4 of the pepper/onion mixture on top of each tortilla. Add a little salsa, cheese, and top with sour cream.

SPAGHETTI SQUASH PISELLI WITH SAUCE

1 medium spaghetti squash	1/4 fresh basil, chopped or 3 tbsp. dried
16 oz. peas, frozen	1 can 14.5 oz. diced tomatoes
2 tbsp. olive oil	Salt and pepper to taste
2 large onions, sliced long, not chopped	1 tbsp. garlic powder
4 cloves fresh garlic, chopped	2 tbsp. grated cheese (optional)

Wash spaghetti squash. No need to cut. Cook in oven in shallow dish at 400 F for 50 minutes. It will be hot, so hold squash with oven mitt or paper towel.

Cut spaghetti squash lengthwise. Hold one end with hand and with a fork take the seeds and pulp out. Can throw out the seeds, or save and bake like you would pumpkin seeds, in oven. Hold the squash upright inside a large bowl.

With a fork, scrape from top to bottom bringing the squash into the bowl. Continue this with both halves. Cover to keep warm.

Heat oil on medium-high heat. Add onions and sauté until translucent. Add garlic and cook for 1 minute more. Add diced tomatoes, (including 1/2 can of water), basil, and seasonings. Lower to medium heat.

Add peas. Cover and cook for 8 minutes.

Place a little of the sauce mixture on bottom of a serving platter. Add some spaghetti squash. Continue this way mixing as you go. Top off with a little grated cheese if you desire.

** This is one of my most favorite dishes. Can be served as a main dish with a salad or a side dish.

STUFFED PEPPERS

1 c. quinoa, uncooked
8 medium green peppers,
   tops removed and seeded
1 large onion, chopped
2 garlic cloves, minced
2 6 oz. cans of black olives,
   sliced
2 tbsp. olive oil

1 28 oz. can diced tomatoes,
   drained
1 12 oz. jar of mild, medium
   or hot salsa
12 oz. mozzarella cheese,
   shredded

Cook quinoa according to directions. Steam peppers until soft but not limp.

In a large skillet, sauté the onion and garlic in oil on medium heat. Add the diced tomatoes, salsa and black olives. Cook for 10 minutes.

Mix in the quinoa, lower heat, and simmer for another 5 minutes. Place peppers in a baking dish and fill the peppers with the quinoa mixture.

Sprinkle the cheese over the peppers and bake at 325 F for 35 minutes.

It's not your position that makes you happy,
it is your disposition.
- O.S. Marden

Breads, Loaves & Muffins

OVEN TEMPERATURE CHART

Low	250-325F
Moderate	325-375F
Moderate Hot	375-425F
Hot	425-450F
Very Hot	450-475F

TEMPERATURES FOR BAKING

FOOD	Temp.	Time
Butter Cake, loaf	360-400F	40-60 min.
Butter Cake, layer	380-400F	20-40 min.
Cake, fruit	275-325F	3-4 hrs.
Cookies, thin	380-390F	10-12 min.
Cookies, molasses	350-375F	18-20 min.
Cream Puffs	300-350F	45-60 min.
Meringues	250-300F	40-60 min.
Pie Crust	400-500F	20-40 min.

CAKES	Temp.	Time
Angel	325F	60 min.
Sponge	325F	60 min.
Cup	350F	25 min.
Layer	375F	25-30 min.
Loaf	350F	45-60 min.
Sheet	375F	20-30 min.
Pound	325F	60-90 min.

PIES	Temp.	Time
Pumpkin	400F	35-45 min.
Two-crust	400F	25-40 min.
Shells	450F	10-12 min.
Meringue	300F	10-15 min.

ROUND ITALIAN HERB BREAD

2 3/4 c. almond flour
1/4 tsp. sea salt
1 1/2 tsp. baking soda
1 tsp. dried basil
1 tsp. garlic powder
1 tsp. dried oregano
1 tsp. onion powder

1/4 c. freshly grated asiago cheese
2 eggs
2 tbsp. apple cider vinegar
1 tbsp. olive oil
Coarse sea salt to sprinkle on top to taste

In a large bowl, combine flour, salt, baking soda, basil, garlic, oregano, onion powder and cheese.

In a smaller bowl blend together, eggs, and apple cider vinegar. Mix the wet ingredients into the dry.

Place dough on a baking sheet lined with parchment paper or silicone mat. Form dough into a circle that is 8 inch wide and 1 1/2 inch deep. Drizzle the olive oil all over the dough, including the bottom. Sprinkle salt on top.

Using a serrated knife, cut the top of the dough 1/2 inch deep, in the shape of an x. Bake at 350 F for 20 minutes. Turn oven off and leave bread in oven for 10 minutes more. Cool a little before serving.

ALMOND FLOUR BREAD

1 1/2 c. almond flour
3/4 c. arrowroot flour
1/4 c. flax seed meal
1/2 tsp. sea salt

1/2 tsp. baking soda
4 eggs
2 tsp. xylitol
1 tsp. apple cider vinegar

In a medium size bowl, combine almond flour, arrowroot, flax meal, salt and baking soda.

In a larger bowl, blend eggs 3 to 4 minutes until frothy. Stir xylitol and vinegar into eggs. Mix dry ingredients into wet ingredients. Pour batter into a well greased 7.5 x 3.5 inch loaf pan. Bake at 350 F for 30 to 35 minutes, or until inserted toothpick, into center of loaf, comes out clean.

GLAZED PUMPKIN SPICE WALNUT LOAF
Loaf:

1 c. almond flour
1/4 c. coconut flour
1/2 tsp. baking soda
1 tbsp. cinnamon
1/2 tsp. pumpkin pie spice
3 packets stevia
3 eggs

1 tsp. apple cider vinegar
1 1/2 tsp. vanilla
1/2 c. pumpkin purée
1 tbsp. grapeseed oil
1 c. walnuts, chopped
Coconut oil to lightly oil pan

In a large bowl mix first 6 ingredients. In a medium bowl beat eggs. Blend in vinegar. Add vanilla, pumpkin and grapeseed oil. Mix well.

Add wet ingredients to dry ingredients and mix well. Fold in walnuts. Pour into oiled loaf pan and bake at 325 F for 30 to 35 minutes, or until toothpick comes out clean. Put on cooling rack to cool completely before cutting.

Pumpkin Spice Glaze:

1 tbsp. honey
1 tbsp. coconut butter
2 tbsp. canned coconut milk

1 tsp. butter
1/8 tsp. pumpkin spice
1/2 tsp. vanilla extract

Mix all ingredients in a blender and purée. Leave at room temperature until ready to glaze.

When loaf is completely cooled, spread a thin layer of glaze on top of the loaf and then drizzle the rest of the glaze over the top.

SANDWICH/FLATBREAD

1 1/2 c. almond flour	3 eggs
3/4 c. tapioca flour	1/3 c. plain yogurt,
1/3 c. chia seeds	full or low fat
1 tsp. xylitol	1/4 tsp. garlic powder
1/2 tsp. baking soda	1/4 tsp. onion powder
1/2 tsp. sea salt	1/4 tsp. black pepper

In a large bowl, combine almond flour, tapioca, chia, xylitol, baking soda and salt.

In a smaller bowl, blend eggs and yogurt with an electric mixer just until mixed.

Add the egg mixture into the dry ingredients. Continue to use mixer to combine, until it forms a sticky, wet dough. Pour batter into a 12x16 inch cookie sheet lined with parchment paper, or a silicone baking mat. Smooth batter out with a spatula over the entire surface area, making it thin and even.

Mix together garlic powder, onion powder and black pepper. Sprinkle over dough. Bake at 350 F for 8 minutes or until toothpick comes out clean. Do not overbake.

If making flatbread, add toppings and heat in oven until done. If making sandwiches, cut into sandwich size slices. Store in parchment paper.

** This delicious bread is great for sandwiches, for dipping, or a flatbread with toppings.

Learn from the mistakes of others. You cannot live long enough to make them all yourself.
- John Luther

NUT BREAD

1 1/2 c. almond flour
3/4 c. arrowroot flour
1/4 c. flaxseed meal
1/2 tsp. sea salt
1/2 tsp. baking soda
4 eggs

1 tsp. xylitol
1 tsp. apple cider vinegar
1/4 c. walnuts, chopped
1/4 c. cashews, chopped
1/2 c. pumpkin seeds

In a medium bowl, combine almond flour, arrowroot, flaxseed meal, salt and baking soda.

In a large bowl, beat or whisk eggs, 3 to 5 minutes or until frothy. Stir xylitol and vinegar into eggs. Mix dry ingredients into wet. Fold in nuts and seeds. Pour batter into a well greased loaf baking dish.

Bake at 350 F for 30 to 35 minutes or until inserted toothpick comes out clean.

PECAN CRANBERRY SPONGE LOAF

1/2 c. quinoa flour
1/4 tsp. sea salt
1 tsp. baking soda
3 eggs
1/2 c. grapeseed oil

1/4 c. honey & 4 drops liquid
stevia
1 tbsp. vanilla extract
3/4 c. pecans, chopped
1 1/4 c. frozen cranberries,
thawed

Place quinoa flour, salt, and baking soda in food processor or high powered blender. Pulse ingredients together. Pulse in eggs, grapeseed oil, honey, stevia and vanilla. Fold in cranberries and pecans.

Pour batter into a greased 9x5 inch loaf pan. Bake at 350 F for 35 minutes or until inserted toothpick comes out clean.

** This loaf is really light and spongy. You will enjoy the texture, as much as the taste.

CINNAMON RAISIN BREAD

1/4 c. (1/2 stick butter)
2 tbsp. honey
5 eggs
1/8 tsp. sea salt
1/2 tsp. baking soda
1 tsp. vanilla
2 tbsp. ground cinnamon
1/2 tsp. nutmeg

1 tbsp. grapeseed oil
1/3 c. coconut oil
1 tsp. apple cider vinegar
3/4 c. almond flour
3/4 c. raisins
1 tbsp. butter,
   to grease loaf dish

Melt butter in a small saucepan over low heat. Turn off heat. Add honey and stir. Set aside.

In a large bowl, combine the eggs, salt, baking soda, vanilla, cinnamon, nutmeg, grapeseed oil, and vinegar. Blend well with high powdered blender, or hand mixer. Add the butter and honey, and combine. Fold in the raisins. Butter the loaf dish. Pour batter into loaf dish. Bake at 325 F for 40 minutes or until inserted toothpick comes out clean.

HONEY BISCUITS

2 1/2 c. almond flour
1/2 tsp. sea salt
1/2 tsp. baking soda
1/4 c. grapeseed oil
1/4 c. honey

2 eggs
1 tsp. butter,
   at room temperature
1 tbsp. butter,
   for greasing baking sheet

In a large bowl, combine almond flour, salt and baking soda.

In a medium bowl, whisk together oil, honey, eggs and butter. Stir wet ingredients into the dry. Mix completely.

Line parchment paper or silicone mat on baking sheet. generously grease with butter.

Fill ice cream scoop with batter and drop onto baking sheet. Bake at 350 F for 15 minutes, or until golden brown.

CRANBERRY ALMOND LOAF

1/4 c. (1/2 stick butter)	1 tbsp. grapeseed oil
3 tbsp. honey	1/3 c. coconut flour
5 eggs, room temperature	1/4 c. almond flour
1/4 tsp. sea salt	5 oz. dried cranberries
1/4 tsp. baking soda	5 oz. sliced almonds
1 tsp. vanilla	1 tbsp. coconut oil, to grease
1 tsp. cinnamon	loaf pan

Melt butter in a small saucepan over low heat. Remove from heat. Add honey and stir. In a large bowl, combine the eggs, salt, baking soda, vanilla, cinnamon, and grapeseed oil. Blend well with high powered blender, or hand mixer. Add in the butter and honey. Add the coconut flour and almond flour to the large bowl. Blend completely with other ingredients. Fold in the cranberries and almonds.

Heavily grease loaf dish with coconut oil and pour batter into loaf dish. Bake at 325 F for 40 minutes, or until inserted toothpick comes out clean.

CHEESY BISCUITS

1/4 c. butter, melted	1/4 tsp. baking soda
3 medium eggs	1 c. sharp Cheddar cheese,
1/3 c. coconut flour	shredded
1/4 tsp. salt	2 tbsp. butter to grease cookie
1/4 tsp. garlic powder	sheet

In a medium size bowl, whisk together eggs and butter. In a small bowl, mix together coconut flour, salt, garlic powder and baking soda. Whisk dry ingredients into wet. Continue to whisk until no lumps. Fold in cheese.

Line cookie sheet with parchment paper or silicone mat. Grease with butter. Use an ice cream scoop to drop batter onto greased cookie sheet. Bake at 400 F for 10 to 15 minutes, or until golden brown. Let cool a bit before serving. Cool completely before storing to keep them crisp.

CRISPY THYME CRACKERS

2 c. almond flour

1/3 c. sunflower seeds

1 tsp. fresh thyme leaves, chopped

1 tsp. salt

1/2 tsp. fresh ground black pepper

4 tsp. olive oil

1/4 c. cold water

1/8 tsp. dried thyme (optional), for top

1/2 tsp. fresh ground pepper, for top

In a large bowl, add all ingredients (except 1/8 teaspoon dried thyme and 1/2 teaspoon pepper, to sprinkle on top). With gloved or clean hands, combine all ingredients until thoroughly mixed, and forms a ball. Cut the ball in half so there are two separate balls.

Place one ball between two pieces of parchment paper. Roll dough out until it is 1/8 inch thick or less, and even, especially at the ends, so not to burn. Remove top piece of parchment paper. Sprinkle on top, pepper, and dried thyme (optional). Cut dough with a knife or pizza cutter into cracker size pieces. Transfer the dough and the parchment paper, onto a baking sheet. Bake at 350 F for 10 minutes or until light golden brown. Repeat with second ball of dough.

APPLE MUFFINS

2 1/2 c. almond flour

1 tsp. cinnamon

1/2 tsp. sea salt

1/2 tsp. baking soda

1/4 c. grapeseed oil

1/4 c. honey

1 tsp. vanilla

2 eggs

1 tsp. apple cider vinegar

1 c. Granny Smith apples, cored, peeled, chopped

In a large bowl, combine almond flour, cinnamon, salt and baking soda. In a medium bowl, whisk together oil, honey, vanilla, egg, and vinegar. Stir wet ingredients into the dry. Mix completely. Fold in apples. Pour batter into muffin pans or silicone muffin cups, 3/4 filled. Bake at 350 F for 20 minutes, or until inserted toothpick comes out clean.

MULTI - SEED CRACKERS

1/4 c. sesame seeds
1/4 c. pumpkin seeds
1/4 c. sunflower seeds
1/4 c. chia seeds

1/2 c. warm water
1/4 tsp. sea salt
Enough oil to lightly grease
  baking sheet

Place chia and sesame seeds in a medium mixing bowl and stir to combine evenly.

Note: These two small seeds need to be mixed first to prevent clumping. Add remaining seeds and combine evenly. Stir salt into warm water until dissolved. Add water to seeds and stir well. Water will absorb in a minute and mixture will thicken.

Line baking sheet with parchment paper or silicone mat. Oil lightly. Spread seed mixture evenly, about 1/8 inch thick or thinner. Bake at 325 F for 30 minutes. Remove from oven and flip over. Add more salt if desire. Cut into squares and bake for another 15 minutes.

CRACKED PEPPER CRANBERRY CRACKERS

2 c. almond flour
1/4 c. sunflower seeds
3/4 c. dried cranberries
1 tsp. salt
1/2 tsp. fresh cracked pepper

1/4 c. cold water
4 tsp. olive oil
Cracked pepper
  to sprinkle on top

Add all ingredients (except some pepper) to a food processor or a high powered blender. Process until well combined. Form a ball with the dough. Cut the ball in half so there are two separate balls.

Place one ball between two pieces of parchment paper. Roll dough out until it is 1/8 inch thick, or less, and even, especially at ends, so not to burn. Remove top piece of parchment paper. Sprinkle pepper on top. Cut dough with a knife or pizza cutter into cracker size pieces. Transfer the dough and the parchment paper onto a baking sheet. Bake at 350 F for 10 minutes or until light golden brown. Repeat with second ball of dough.

DONIVAN'S
LEMON POPPY SEED MUFFINS

1/2 c. coconut flour	1/2 tbsp. vanilla extract
1/4 tsp. baking soda	1 large lemon, the juice and the zest
1/4 tsp. sea salt	
6 eggs	1 tbsp. poppy seeds or chia seeds
1/2 c. butter, melted	
1/3 c. honey	Butter to grease muffin cups

In a small bowl mix the coconut flour, baking soda and salt.

In a large bowl, with a hand mixer, blend eggs, butter, honey, vanilla, lemon juice and zest. Be sure not to zest the white part of lemon or muffins will taste bitter. Mix dry ingredients into wet. Blend well. Stir in poppy seeds or chia seeds.

Grease muffin paper cups or silicone cups and place into muffin tray. Fill each muffin cup 3/4's full with batter.

Bake at 350 F for 30 minutes, or until inserted toothpick comes out clean.

PUMPKIN MUFFINS

1 1/4 c. almond flour	2 large eggs
1/4 c. coconut flour	2 tbsp. coconut oil, liquid
1/2 tsp. baking soda	1/3 c. honey
1/2 tsp. sea salt	4 drops of liquid stevia
1 tsp. cinnamon	1 1/2 c. canned pumpkin purée
2 tsp. pumpkin pie spice	

In a large bowl, mix together, flours, baking soda, salt, cinnamon and pumpkin pie spice.

In a separate bowl, use a hand mixer to blend eggs, oil, honey, stevia and pumpkin. Add dry ingredients to wet and mix until thoroughly combined. Pour batter into muffin pan lined with paper or silicone cups. Bake at 350 F for 30 minutes or until inserted toothpick comes out clean.

EXTRA RECIPES:

_____

_____

_____

_____

_____

_____

_____

_____

_____

_____

_____

_____

_____

_____

_____

Cakes & Desserts

OVEN TEMPERATURE CHART

MISCELLANEOUS	Temp.	Minutes
Custard Cup	300F	20-30
Custard Casserole	300F	45-60
Soufflé	325F	50-60
Timbales	300F	35-45
Rice Pudding	325F	50-60

TABLE FOR DRIED FRUITS

FRUIT	Amount of Sugar or Honey	Cooking Time
Apricots	1/4 c. for each c. fruit	40 min.
Figs	1 tbsp. for each c. fruit	30 min.
Peaches	1/4 c. for each c. fruit	45 min.
Prunes	2 tbsp. for each c. fruit	45 min.

RULES FOR WHIPPING CREAM

- Chill the cream, bowl and beaters in a refrigerator for at least 2 hours. Beat until it is fairly stiff.
- If cream is beaten until it is warmer than 45 degrees, it will turn to butter.
- Should cream start to turn buttery, whip in 2 or 3 more tbsp. of cold milk.
- If you wish the cream to keep stiff for a day or two, add one teaspoon gelatine soaked in one tablespoon cold water. Dissolve the gelatine over hot water; allow to cool to the consistency of egg white before adding to the cream and whipping.
- Use medium speed when whipping cream with an electric beater.
- Cream, when whipped, almost doubles in bulk.

SUBSTITUTES FOR WHIPPING CREAM

1. Use light cream or cereal cream after allowing it to stand undisturbed for 48 hours in the refrigerator. Whip as you would whipping cream.
2. Prepare cream as given above. Soak 1 tsp. gelatine in 2 tbsp. cold water and dissolve over hot water. Allow to cool; then add to the cream and whip.
3. Use evaporated milk. Milk prepared with gelatine holds up better and longer, but may be more convenient to chill it on occasion. Chill 12 hours. Use medium speed on the electric beater when whipping.

CHOCOLATE CRANBERRY LAYER CAKE WITH CHOCOLATE FROSTING

Chocolate Cranberry Cake:

5 medium eggs, at room temperature
1 tbsp. vanilla extact
1 c. honey
1/2 c. butter, melted
1/2 c. coconut oil, melted or in liquid state
1 1/4 c. + 2 tbsp. almond flour
1 c. natural carob powder
1/2 tsp. baking soda
1 1/2 c. frozen cranberries, thawed

In a large bowl, combine eggs, vanilla, honey, butter and coconut oil. Beat or mix until smooth.

In a separate bowl add almond flour, carob, and baking soda. Stir to blend. Add to egg mixture and mix until smooth. Fold in cranberries.

Pour batter into 2 greased 9 inch glass cake baking dishes. You can also put parchment paper on top of greased baking dish to assure that cake will not stick to dish.

Bake at 350 F for 35 minutes or until inserted toothpick comes out clean. Cool cakes on wire rack completely before frosting. Frost each layer and sides with a spatula. For best results place frosted cake in refrigerator for at least 20 minutes or until serving.

Frosting:

4 cans coconut milk, full fat, chilled
1 medium pot or bowl, chilled
2/3 c. natural carob
1 tsp. vanilla
4 drops of liquid stevia

Open the 4 cans of canned coconut milk and separate the solid from the liquid.

Put the solid part into the chilled bowl from the freezer. The liquid can be used at another time for smoothies, recipes, etc.

Add the carob, vanilla and stevia. Whisk together. Refrigerate until ready to frost cake.

ORANGE COCONUT 4 LAYER CAKE

Orange Coconut Cake:

10 eggs, at room temperature
1 tbsp. vanilla extract
1/4 tsp. liquid stevia
1/2 c. xylitol
1 c. coconut oil, melted
2 tsp. orange zest

3/4 c. coconut flour
1 tsp. sea salt
1 tsp. baking soda
1 c. shredded coconut
1 orange,
    to juice into holes at each
    layer

In a large bowl, beat together eggs, vanilla, stevia, xylitol, melted oil and orange zest. In a small bowl add coconut flour, salt and baking soda.

Add dry ingredients into wet and continue to blend. When batter is smooth, stir in shredded coconut.

Grease two 9 inch cake dishes generously with coconut oil. (You may put parchment paper over the oil before pouring batter so cake does not stick to dish.) Pour batter into dishes. Bake at 325 F for 35 minutes or until inserted toothpick comes out clean. Cool.

Slice each cake horizontally to create 4 layers of cake.

Before you frost each layer, poke holes in each layer of cake with a fork. and Juice the orange over each layer as you go.

Orange Coconut Frosting:

4 cans full fat coconut milk,
    chilled
1 medium size bowl chilled
    from freezer
1/4 tsp. liquid stevia

2 tsp. xylitol
1 1/2 tsp. vanilla extract
1 tsp. orange zest
1/2 c. shredded coconut
1/4 c. coconut flakes
    (optional)

Open each can of coconut milk and take out the solid part and put in the chilled bowl from freezer. Pour the liquid part into a jar. (The liquid will not be used for this recipe, although can be used at another time for smoothies, sauces, etc.)

Continued...

Add to the bowl with the coconut milk, stevia, xylitol, vanilla and orange zest. Whisk until combined. Fold in shredded coconut with a spatula. With the spatula generously frost each layer, sides and top with frosting. Sprinkle the coconut flakes on sides and top.

** I love this 4 layer cake. It's great for parties.

*Note: Prepare a medium size pot or bowl chilled in freezer and 4 cans of coconut milk in refrigerator.

CHOCOLATE LAYER CAKE
WITH CHOCOLATE DATE FROSTING

5 eggs, at room temperature
1 tbsp. vanilla extract
1 c. honey
1/2 c. butter, melted

1/2 c. coconut oil,
**   melted or in liquid state**
1 1/4 c. + 2 tbsp. almond flour
1 c. carob
1/2 tsp. baking soda

In a large bowl, combine eggs, vanilla, honey, butter, and coconut oil. Beat or mix until smooth.

Add almond flour, carob and baking soda. Stir to blend. Grease two 9 inch round cake dishes. (You may put parchment paper over oil before pouring batter, so cake does not stick to dish.)

Bake at 350 F for 25 minutes or until inserted toothpick comes out clean. Cool completely. Cut both cakes horizontally to create 4 layers of cake. Frost each layer and sides with frosting using a spatula. For best results put frosted cake in refrigerator until serving.

Frosting:
1 c. vanilla almond milk
1 c. soaked cashew nuts
1/3 c. brazil nuts
1 tsp. vanilla extract

2/3 c. dates
3 tbsp. all natural carob
**   powder**

Mix all ingredients in a high powered blender or food processor. Process until it's a frosting consistency. Refrigerate until ready to frost cake.

CARROT CAKE
Cake:

3/4 c. coconut flour
1 tbsp. cinnamon
1 tsp. baking soda
1/2 tsp. sea salt
10 eggs
1 tsp. vanilla
1 c. coconut oil, melted

1/2 c. honey
1 tsp. stevia
6 carrots, peeled,
   shredded & sliced in half
1 c. walnuts, chopped
1/4 c. shredded coconut
   (optional)

In a medium bowl, combine coconut flour, cinnamon, baking soda, and salt.

In a large bowl, use a hand mixer to blend eggs, vanilla, coconut oil, honey and stevia. Add dry ingredients to wet, and mix completely.

Mix the shredded carrots into batter. Fold walnuts into batter. Fold shredded coconut into batter (optional).

Grease two 9 inch cake dishes with coconut oil. Bake at 325 F for 35 minutes, or until inserted toothpick comes out clean.

Let cakes cool completely. Slice both cakes horizontally, to make 4 layers.

Frost each layer, sides, and top of cake with the cream cheese frosting.

Cream Cheese Frosting:

3 8 oz. pkg. cream cheese,
   softened
3/4 c. butter, softened

1 1/4 tsp. vanilla
4 tbsp. honey
4 drops of liquid stevia

In a large bowl, use a hand mixer to blend cream cheese and butter, until creamy. Mix in vanilla. Gradually, stir in honey and stevia. Blend thoroughly.

Refrigerate until cake is cool, and you are ready to frost.

DEEP DISH LEMON/LIME CHEESECAKE

Pie Crust:

5 c. almond flour   1 c. butter, melted
1/2 tsp. sea salt   3 tbsp. honey
1 tsp. baking soda   4 tbsp. vanilla extract

In a large bowl, combine flour, salt and baking soda. In a medium bowl, combine butter, honey and vanilla. Pour wet ingredients into dry and mix completely. Press the dough into the bottom and up the sides of a 9 1/2 inch deep dish pie plate.

Bake at 325 F for 10 minutes, or until lightly golden. Let cool completely before filling with cheesecake filling and baking again.

Cheesecake Filling:

8 oz. cream cheese,   1/2 lemon or lime, the juice
    at room temperature   and the zest
16 oz. full-fat Greek yogurt   1/2 c. honey
1 tsp. vanilla extract   1/2 tsp. sea salt
    4 eggs

Combine cheesecake ingredients (except for the eggs) in a large bowl. Do not zest the white part of lime nor lemon, or it will be bitter. Whisk, and then blend eggs one at a time into the mix. With a hand mixer blend until smooth.

Pour mixture over the crust.

Bake at 350 F for 55 minutes, or until crust is a golden brown and the filling is set and golden. Cool. Chill well before serving.

Be happy for no reason like a child. If you are happy for a reason, it can be taken from you.
- Deepak Chopra

NEW YORK ALMOND CHEESECAKE

**8 oz. cream cheese,
    at room temperature**
16 oz. full fat Greek yogurt
1 tsp. vanilla extract
1/2 tsp. almond extract

1/2 c. honey
1/2 tsp. sea salt
4 eggs
1/4 c. sliced almonds

In a large bowl, combine all ingredients (except the eggs and almonds). Blend well with a hand mixer. Blend eggs into the mix, one at a time. Blend until smooth.

Pour batter into a 9 1/2 x 1 1/2 inch Corning ware pie dish. Top with almonds. Bake at 350 F for 50 minutes or until set and edges are light golden brown.

CHOCOLATE CUPCAKES
WITH VANILLA CINNAMON GLAZE

6 medium eggs
**1/2 c. coconut oil,
    melted or in liquid state**
1/2 c. butter, melted
1/3 tsp. liquid stevia
1 c. honey

1 tbsp. vanilla extract
1 tsp. apple cider vinegar
1 1/4 c. + 2 tbsp. almond flour
1/2 tsp. baking soda
1 c. natural carob

In a large bowl, combine eggs, oil, butter, stevia, honey, vanilla, and vinegar. Beat or mix until smooth.

In a separate bowl add almond flour, baking soda and carob. Stir to blend. Mix dry ingredients into wet. Blend completely.

Pour batter into greased muffin pans or silicone cups. Bake at 350 F for 25 minutes or until toothpick comes out clean.

Cool completely. Frost with vanilla cinnamon glaze from this and that section.

** Made with carob that is naturally caffeine free.

RASPBERRY VANILLA CUPCAKES
WITH FROSTING

1/2 c. coconut flour	1/4 c. grapeseed oil
1 tbsp. arrowroot flour	1/2 c. honey
1/4 tsp. sea salt	1 tbsp. vanilla extract
1/2 tsp. baking soda	3/4 c. raspberries, chopped
4 large eggs	Grapeseed oil for greasing

In a medium bowl mix flours, salt and baking soda. In a large bowl blend together eggs, grapeseed oil, honey and vanilla. Mix dry ingredients into wet, blending with the mixer as you go.

Gently fold in the raspberries. Place greased paper muffin cups or silicone cups into a muffin pan. Fill each cup 3/4 full. Bake at 350 F for 20 minutes or until inserted toothpick comes out clean.

Vanilla Raspberry Frosting:

2 cans full fat coconut milk, chilled in refrigerator	2 tsp. xylitol
	1/4 c. raspberries, whole
1 tbsp. vanilla	

Place medium size bowl in freezer to get cold.

In cold bowl place only the solid portion of the coconut milk. The liquid part can be used at another time for making smoothies, sauces, etc. Add vanilla and xylitol. Whisk together until it forms stiff peaks. Gently fold in raspberries. Place on top of each muffin.

Circumstance does not make the man; it reveals him to himself.
– James Allen

COCONUT MACAROONS

2 egg whites
1/4 c. honey
Dash of sea salt
1/2 tsp. vanilla

1 c. unsweetened shredded
coconut
1 tbsp. butter for greasing
baking sheet

In a large bowl, beat egg whites until stiff peaks form. Gradually fold in honey, salt, vanilla, and coconut.

Coat cooking sheet with a generous amount of butter. Drop by the rounded teaspoon onto baking sheet lined with parchment paper or silicone mat.

Bake at 325 F for 15 minutes, or until edges are lightly browned and crispy.

** These are so good you may want to make a double batch.

NANA PARADISO'S ITALIAN SESAME COOKIES

1 1/2 c. almond flour
1/2 tsp. baking soda
3 tbsp. xylitol
3 tsp. butter, room
temperature
2 eggs, medium

4 drops liquid stevia
1 tbsp. vanilla extract
1 tbsp. honey
1/2 tsp. apple cider vinegar
1/2 c. sesame seeds,
hulled or unhulled, in a dish

In a large bowl mix flour, baking soda, xylitol and butter. Blend completely. Make a well in the center of the dough.

In a separate bowl beat eggs, stevia, vanilla, honey and apple cider vinegar. Pour the wet ingredients into the well of the dough and mix together completely. The dough should not be dry.

Take a tablespoon of dough and roll it in your hands, making an almond shape. Roll dough in the dish with the sesame seeds, covering the dough. Place cookies on baking sheet lined with parchment paper or silicone mat. Flatten the dough a little with your hands. Bake at 425 F for 10 minutes or until golden brown.

CHIANNE'S HONEY SESAME COOKIES

1 1/2 c. almond flour
1/2 tsp. baking soda
2 eggs
1/4 c. honey

3 tsp. butter
1 tbsp. vanilla extract
1/2 c. sesame seeds, hulled or
    unhulled in a dish

In a large bowl, combine almond flour and baking soda.

In a smaller bowl, beat eggs, honey, butter and vanilla. Pour egg mixture into dry ingredients. Mix completely. Dough should not be dry.

Form dough into 1 inch balls. Roll into sesame seeds.

Place on baking sheet lined with parchment paper or silicone mat. Flatten out. Bake at 425 F for 10 minutes or until golden brown.

COOKIE PRESS COOKIES

2 1/2 c. almond flour
1/2 tsp. baking soda
1/2 c. xylitol
1 stick of butter,
    room temperature

2 eggs
1 tbsp. vanilla extract
1/2 tsp. apple cider vinegar

In a large bowl mix flour, baking soda, and xylitol. Beat in butter with the dry ingredients and knead it together. Make a well in the middle of dry ingredients.

In a separate bowl, beat eggs, vanilla and apple cider vinegar. Gradually mix the eggs and vanilla in the well you made with the dough. Mix all the ingredients together and knead the dough until you see holes. Cover the pot and let sit for 1 hour.

Fill cookie press with the dough and turn out cookies 1 to 2 inches apart onto a baking sheet with a silicone mat.

Bake at 350 F for 15 minutes or until golden brown. Cool before serving.

COOKIE CUTTER COOKIES
WITH VANILLA CINNAMON ICING

Cookies:

3 c. almond flour

1/4 tsp. sea salt

1/4 tsp. baking soda

1/8 tsp. nutmeg

1/2 c. coconut oil, melted

1/4 c. honey

1 tbsp. lemon zest

In a large bowl, mix almond flour, salt, baking soda and nutmeg. In a small bowl, mix coconut oil, honey and lemon zest. Add wet ingredients to dry and mix completely.

Make a ball with the dough and cut the ball in half to form two separate balls. Put each ball between two pieces of parchment paper.

Roll each ball out to 1/8 inch thickness. Place both in freezer for 30 minutes to chill. This is important because the dough will stick to the cutter if not chilled.

When chilled, take top parchment paper off and put cookie cutter on top of dough and press. There will be pieces of dough left over. Make another ball out of the left over dough, roll it out, and put in freezer again. Put cookies on a silicone lined baking sheet.

Bake at 350 F for about 5 minutes. Keep your eyes on them, they cook pretty fast. Cool completely before putting icing on them. When iced, store in refrigerator so icing hardens a bit.

Vanilla Cinnamon Icing:

1 tbsp. honey

1 tbsp. and 1 tsp. coconut oil, hardened

1 tbsp. butter, cold

1/4 tsp. ground cinnamon

1/2 tsp. vanilla extract

In a blender, processor or hand mixer, blend all ingredients until puréed.

Keep icing at room temperature until cookies are cooled and you are ready to put the icing on them.

** This recipe can be used with any cookie cutter design.

LEMON CHIVÁN BISCOTTI

1 1/4 c. almond flour	1/4 c. xylitol
1 tbsp. arrowroot flour	1 tbsp. lemon zest
1/4 tsp. sea salt	1/4 c. toasted almonds, sliced
1/4 tsp. baking soda	

In a food processor or high powered blender, combine almond flour, arrowroot flour, salt, and baking soda. Pulse until ingredients are well combined.

Add xylitol and continue to pulse until the dough forms a ball.

Remove dough and place in a bowl. Add sliced almonds and lemon zest. Be careful not to zest white part of lemon. It will make the lemon bitter. Form dough into 2 logs on a baking sheet lined with parchment paper or a silicone mat.

Bake at 350 F for 15 minutes. Remove from oven and cool for 1 hour. Cut logs into 1/2 inch slices on a diagonal with a sharp knife. Spread slices out on the baking sheet and bake at 300 F for 15 minutes. As they cool they will become crispy.

** These Lemon Biscotti's are my daughter Chiván's favorite, hence the name.

CASHEW BUTTER COOKIES

1 egg	1/3 c. xylitol
1 tsp. almond extract	6 drops liquid stevia
1/4 tsp. sea salt	1 c. cashew butter

With an electric mixer, beat the egg, almond extract, salt, xylitol, and stevia. Add cashew butter and continue to mix thoroughly.

Line a cookie sheet with parchment paper or silicone mat. Measure 1 tablespoon amount of dough and form a ball. Place on cookie sheet. Gently flatten with a fork, horizontally and then vertically, making a crisscross design. Bake at 350 F for 12 minutes. Cool completely and treat gently. Store in an airtight container or wrapped in parchment paper.

PUMPKIN ICED COOKIES

2 1/2 c. almond flour	2 tsp. pumpkin spice
2 tbsp. coconut flour	1 egg
1/2 tsp. baking soda	1/2 c. pumpkin purée
1/8 tsp. of sea salt	1/3 c. of honey
1 tsp. ground cinnamon	1 tsp. vanilla

In a medium size bowl, mix together, flours, baking soda, salt, and spices.

In a separate bowl, beat the egg, pumpkin purée, honey and vanilla. Slowly mix the dry ingredients into the wet while you are still mixing, or beating.

Scoop a small melon scoop size amount of dough onto a baking sheet lined with parchment paper or silicone mat. Press with back of scoop to flatten cookies slightly. Bake at 350 F for 18 minutes. Cool completely before icing.

Pumpkin Spice Icing:

1 tbsp. honey	1 tbsp. butter, cold
1 tbsp. coconut oil, in solid state	1/4 tsp. ground cinnamon
	1/2 tsp. pumpkin spice

In a blender, processor or hand mixer, blend all ingredients until puréed.

Keep icing at room temperature until cookies are completely cooled and are ready to be iced.

You are the source of all your emotions. At any moment you can create or change them.
- Tony Robbins

CHOCOLATE MOUSSE

1 can coconut milk, full fat,
   chilled in refrigerator
1 medium size bowl or pot
   chilled in freezer

1/3 c. natural carob powder
2 tbsp. xylitol
2 c. strawberries,
   whole or sliced

Open chilled coconut milk. The coconut milk will be solid on top and liquid on bottom of can. Spoon out the solid coconut milk and place in the chilled bowl or pot. (Liquid portion can be put in a jar and used for smoothies or cooking at a later time.)

Add carob powder, and xylitol. Whisk until smooth. Place in a covered bowl and refrigerate until serving. Serve with fresh strawberries.

** You can serve with whole strawberries on the side for dipping. You can also serve the mousse layered with strawberry slices. If you desire, top with whipped cream and a large strawberry.

PECAN CRUNCH

1/4 c. unsweetened shredded
   coconut
4 tbsp. cashew butter

4 tbsp. all natural carob
   powder
1/2 c. chopped pecans
2 drops liquid stevia,
   (optional)

Place coconut on a flat plate.

In a medium size bowl, mix cashew butter and carob powder. Fold in the pecans. Add stevia, if using.

Take a teaspoon of the mixture and roll into a ball.

Place mixture into the coconut, and roll to coat evenly. I usually put them into the candy paper cups. You can also place them on parchment paper in an airtight container. Store in freezer or refrigerator.

** This dessert will satisfy your craving for chocolate, using healthy ingredients, and it's caffeine free.

APPLE PIE

Pie Crust:

1/2 c. quinoa flour
2/3 c. arrowroot flour
2/3 c. tapioca flour
1 c. almond flour

1/2 tsp. sea salt
1 1/2 sticks butter, cold
1 large egg, whisked

In a food processor or high powered blender, add the flours and salt. Pulse until well blended. Add cold butter and pulse until it resembles a crumbly mixture. Add egg and pulse until it forms a dough. If dough is too sticky, add a little more arrowroot flour.

Separate dough into 2 even pieces, one for bottom crust and one for the top.

Dust some arrowroot flour between two sheets of parchment paper. Roll dough out into a 10 inch circle. Carefully place dough in pie dish and remove both pieces of parchment paper. Crimp the dough for the crust all along the dish.

Roll the second piece of dough, using the same parchment paper. Set aside.

Pie Filling:

1 tsp. ground cinnamon
1/2 tsp. ground nutmeg
1 tsp. xylitol
6 Granny Smith apples, cored, peeled, sliced 1/4 inch

1 tbsp. butter, melted, to brush on top of crust
Xylitol to sprinkle on top of crust

Combine cinnamon, nutmeg, and xylitol in a large bowl. Add apples and toss to coat.

Spoon apples into pie dish. Place the dough that was set aside, over the filling. Seal, and crimp the edges. Cut 7 slits in the crust. Brush with melted butter. Sprinkle top with xylitol.

Bake at 375 F for 45 minutes or until crust is lightly browned and juice bubbles, through the slits in crust.

WALNUT BROWNIES

5 eggs, at room temperature
1/2 c. coconut oil, melted or in liquid state
1/2 c. butter, melted
3/4 c. honey
1/3 tsp. liquid stevia

1 tbsp. vanilla extract
1 1/2 c. almond flour
1 c. carob
1/2 tsp. baking soda
1/3 c. walnuts, chopped

In a large bowl, combine eggs, oil, butter, honey, stevia and vanilla. Beat or mix until smooth. In a separate bowl, mix together almond flour, carob, and baking soda. Stir to blend. Add dry ingredients into wet and mix well. Fold in some walnuts and leave some for top.

Pour batter into a greased 9 x 13 inch glass baking dish. Top with the remaining walnuts. Bake at 350 F for 21 to 22 minutes or until inserted toothpick comes out clean.

QUINOA PECAN APPLE PIE

1 c. quinoa uncooked
1/2 stick butter
6 Granny Smith apples, cored, peeled, and sliced thin

1/2 c. pecans, chopped
2 egg whites
3 tsp. cinnamon
5 drops liquid stevia

Cook quinoa according to package directions. Set aside. In a large skillet, melt most of the butter, reserving some to grease the pie dish. Add apples, pecans, and 2 teaspoons cinnamon. Sauté until soft. Set aside.

In a medium bowl whisk egg whites. Beat in stevia and 1 tsp. cinnamon. Add cooked quinoa to the egg white mixture and Combine thoroughly.

Grease a 9 inch pie dish. Using most of the quinoa mixture, form a pie crust by pressing the quinoa firmly, to the bottom and up the sides, of the pie dish. Save some quinoa for the top. Bake pie shell at 350 F for 15 minutes. Add apple mixture to pie dish. Form the top crust with remaining quinoa and cinnamon. Bake at 350 F for 30 minutes. Cool and refrigerate before serving for best results.

Teri's Gluten-Free & Grain-Free Healthy Recipes

PUMPKIN PIE

Pumpkin Pie Shell:

1/4 c. almond flour	2 tsp. xylitol
1/2 c. & 1 tbsp. coconut flour	1/4 c. coconut oil, melted
1/4 tsp. sea salt	1 egg
1/4 tsp. baking soda	7 drops liquid stevia
1 tsp. cinnamon	1 tsp. vanilla

Mix the flours, salt, baking soda, cinnamon and xylitol in a medium bowl.

In a small bowl whisk together the oil, egg, stevia, and vanilla. Pour wet ingredients into the dry and mix thoroughly.

Using gloves or clean fingers, press the dough evenly into the bottom and up the sides of a 9 inch pie pan. Bake for 7 minutes, or until it's a very light golden color. Freeze crust for 30 minutes. Meanwhile, you can prepare your filling.

Pumpkin Pie Filling:

1 15 oz. can pumpkin purée	1 tsp. vanilla
1/4 lb. sweet butter, room temperature	1/2 c. canned coconut milk
2 eggs	Pinch of sea salt
2 tsp. cinnamon	2 drops liquid stevia & 2 tsp. xylitol
1/2 tsp. pumpkin pie spice	Whipped cream (optional)

Mix all ingredients (except whipped cream) in food processor or high powered blender. Process until smooth.

Pour into pie shell that you put in the freezer.

Bake at 350 F for 50 minutes. Watch and cover edges, if need. Cool. Refrigerate a few hours before serving. Top off with whipped cream (optional).

This & That

TEN COMMANDMENTS FOR GOOD LIVING

1. **SPEAK TO PEOPLE** - THERE IS NOTHING SO NICE AS A CHEERFUL WORD OF GREETING.

2. **SMILE AT PEOPLE** - IT TAKES 72 MUSCLES TO FROWN AND ONLY 14 TO SMILE.

3. **CALL PEOPLE** - THE SWEETEST MUSIC TO ANYONE'S EARS IS THE SOUND OF HIS/HER OWN NAME.

4. **BE FRIENDLY** AND HELPFUL, IF YOU WOULD HAVE FRIENDS, BE A FRIEND.

5. **BE CORDIAL** - SPEAK AND ACT AS IF EVERYTHING YOU DO IS A GENUINE PLEASURE.

6. **BE GENUINELY** INTERESTED IN PEOPLE - YOU CAN LIKE ALMOST EVERYBODY IF YOU TRY.

7. **BE GENEROUS** WITH PRAISE CAUTIOUS WITH CRITICISM.

8. **BE CONSIDERATE** WITH THE FEELINGS OF OTHERS. THERE ARE USUALLY THREE SIDES TO A CONTROVERSY; YOURS, THE OTHER PERSON'S AND THE RIGHT SIDE.

9. **BE ALERT** TO GIVE SERVICE - WHAT COUNTS MOST IN LIFE IS WHAT WE DO FOR OTHERS.

10. **ADD TO THIS** A GOOD SENSE OF HUMOUR, A BIG DOSE OF PATIENCE PLUS A DASH OF HUMILITY AND YOU WILL BE REWARDED MANY FOLD.

CAULIFLOWER PIZZA

1 head of cauliflower, grated
3 egg whites
1/2 tsp. sea salt
1/2 tsp. garlic powder
4 oz. pizza sauce or tomato sauce
1 tsp. oregano, dried
1 mini sweet yellow pepper, finely sliced

1 mini sweet red pepper, finely sliced
1/2 onion, sliced thin
4 cloves garlic, minced
1/2 c. black olives, sliced
8 fresh basil leaves, small, or chopped
8 oz. fresh mozzarella, whole milk, sliced round

Cook grated cauliflower in a dry skillet over medium heat, stirring constantly, until soft, about 6 minutes. Place cauliflower into a large bowl.

In a small bowl, whisk egg whites, and then add to the cauliflower. Combine thoroughly.

Place parchment paper or silicone mat on a pizza pan or baking sheet. Add cauliflower to the pan, and spread with a spatula to form the pie crust. Sprinkle with sea salt and garlic powder. Cook pie crust at 425 F for 15 minutes or until golden brown.

Top pizza with most of the sauce, leaving an inch around sides.

Evenly distribute the seasonings, toppings, and basil. Top with the mozzarella, and then place a little sauce in spots on top. Place the pie back in the oven. Cook at 425 F for 20 minutes.

** You can also use a high powered blender on pulse to grate the cauliflower, but need to do a little at a time.

You cannot always control what goes on outside, but you can always control what goes on inside.
- Wayne W. Dyer

COCONUT MANGO ICE CREAM

1/3 c. dried mango,
    unsweetened
1/4 c. almond milk

3/4 c. frozen mango
A squeeze of fresh lemon
1/2 c. coconut flakes

Mix the dried mango and milk in a small bowl to soften the mango.

Place the dried mango, milk and all other ingredients into blender. Blend until mixed. If need more milk to move the blender, add a little more. Put in serving bowl and place in freezer for 10 minutes.

Stir mixture and keep in freezer for another 10 minutes, or until ready to serve.

CHOCOLATE FROSTING

2 cans coconut milk, full fat,
    chilled
1 medium pot or bowl, chilled

1/3 c. natural carob
1/2 tsp. vanilla
2 tbsp. xylitol

Open can of coconut milk and separate solid from the liquid form.

Put the solid part into the chilled bowl from freezer. The liquid can be used at another time for smoothies, cooking, etc.

Add the carob, vanilla and xylitol. Whisk together.

Frosting can be used to frost, cakes, cupcakes, etc. Keep in refrigerator until ready to use.

** Tip: If you make cupcakes for children to carry to school, you can cut the cupcake horizontally, put frosting in the middle, and then wrap the whole cupcake.

CASHEW LEMON ICING

1/4 c. raw cashews	3 tsp. water
4 tsp. canned coconut milk	2 tsp. honey, liquid
3 tsp. coconut oil, melted	2 tsp. lemon juice

Add all ingredients to blender or food processor and process until smooth. Wait for the loaf, cookies, etc. to cool before icing.

If you desire, you can spread a thin layer of icing with a spatula on top, then drizzle the rest of the icing.

LEMON GLAZE

1 tbsp. honey	1 tsp. butter
2 tbsp. coconut butter	1 tsp. lemon juice from fresh lemon
2 tbsp. canned coconut milk, full fat	

Mix all ingredients in blender and blend until puréed. Leave at room temperature until ready to glaze. Cool your baked goods, etc. completely before glazing.

If you desire, spread a thin layer with a spatula, on top, then drizzle the rest of the glaze. If you would like the glaze to harden on baked goods, after glazing refrigerate for 15 minutes.

VANILLA CINNAMON GLAZE

1 tbsp. honey	1 tsp. butter
2 tbsp. coconut butter	1/8 tsp. cinnamon
2 tbsp. canned coconut milk	1/2 tsp. vanilla

Mix all ingredients in blender and blend until smooth. Leave at room temperature until ready to glaze.

Cool loaf, cookies, etc. before glazing.

If desire, can spread a thin layer of icing with a spatula on top, then drizzle the rest of the icing. After glazing can refrigerate for 15 minutes, so that the glaze hardens a little.

This & That

CARAMEL APPLES

1 1/2 c. honey	8 Granny Smith apples, cold
1 1/4 c. heavy cream	8 popsicle sticks
1/4 c. butter or coconut oil	Nuts (optional)
3/4 tsp. sea salt	Shredded coconut (optional)

In a large, heavy saucepan, on medium-low heat, bring the honey to just before a boil. There will be bubbles around the edges.

In a separate medium size bowl mix heavy cream, coconut oil and salt. Add heavy cream mix to the honey. Bring to a boil. Once it begins to boil, lower the heat but still keep an active simmer.

Cook for about 14 minutes or until caramel color darkens. As it cools it will thicken. Be patient and allow to thicken a bit.

Put popsicle sticks into apples. Have parchment paper ready. Hold each apple by the stick, and over the pot. Spoon, caramel over the apple.

If using nuts or coconut, put into a dish and dip apple in the dish to coat the bottom and spoon onto the sides. Place caramel apples on the parchment paper to set. When cool, you can place apples into a muffin liner if you desire. Store in refrigerator.

** The caramel can also be used for dipping, topping fruits, ice cream, etc.

Be patient with this recipe and don't cook too high or fast. It can burn quickly.

Loving people live in a loving world. Hostile people live in a hostile world. Same world.
- Wayne W. Dyer

Teri's Gluten-Free & Grain-Free Healthy Recipes

RAW CASHEW CREAM SAUCE AND TOPPING

1 c. raw cashews, whole

Rinse cashews. Put cashews in a bowl with enough water to cover them. Cover the bowl and soak overnight in refrigerator. A short cut is to put the cashews in a pot of water, bring to a boil, then remove from heat and let soak for 1 hour.

Drain, rinse under cold water, and place into a high speed blender or food processor. Add enough water to cover by an inch. For a thicker cream, just use enough water to cover.

Blend for several minutes until smooth and creamy.

** Raw cashews do not have an overbearing taste. This is why it makes the best choice for non-dairy users. You can add ingredients for whatever taste you want. From dessert toppings, fillings, or even Alfredo's. Let your imagination guide you.

DAIRY FREE WHIPPED CREAM

2 cans coconut milk, full fat, chilled in refrigerator

1 medium size bowl or pot, chilled in freezer

1/2 tsp. vanilla

1 tsp. xylitol

1/4 tsp. cinnamon (optional)

Open the cans of coconut milk, and separate the solid part from the liquid.

The liquid can be saved for smoothies, cooking, etc.

Put the solid part in the chilled bowl.

With a hand mixer, beat the cream until it forms soft peaks, about 3 to 5 minutes. Don't over mix or it will turn to butter.

Fold in the xylitol, vanilla, and cinnamon, if you desire.

Refrigerate until you are ready to serve.

CRANBERRY ORANGE SAUCE

1 1/2 oz. pkg. of fresh
   cranberries
1 c. fresh orange juice
1/2 c. honey

1/4 tsp. nutmeg
1/4 tsp. ground cinnamon
1/8 tsp. cloves
1 tsp. orange zest

Mix all ingredients in a saucepan over medium-high heat. Bring
the sauce to a boil. Immediately reduce heat to medium-low
and cook for 15 minutes, or until the berries begin to pop.
Remove from heat. Thickens as it cools.

** This sauce will complement the turkey, green beans, mash
cauliflower, and stuffing recipes found in this recipe book.

ORANGE VINAIGRETTE DRESSING

Juice 1 orange
3 tbsp. extra-virgin olive oil

Cracked black pepper to taste
2 tbsp. orange zest

In a medium size bowl, squeeze the juice from the orange.
Whisk in the oil. Stir in pepper and orange zest.

Toss into a salad of choice.

RANCH DRESSING

1 c. Greek yogurt
1 tsp. apple cider vinegar
1 tbsp. finely chopped Italian
   parsley
1 tsp. finely chopped chives
1/2 tsp. sea salt

1/8 tsp. freshly ground black
   pepper
1 tbsp. fresh dill, minced
1 garlic clove, minced
1/2 tsp. onion powder

Whisk together all ingredients. Cover and place in refrigerator
for 1 hour to bring the flavors together.

Teri's Gluten-Free & Grain-Free Healthy Recipes

CINNAMON RAISIN FRENCH TOAST

4 large eggs	Pinch nutmeg, freshly grated
1/2 c. half and half	Sea salt to taste
1/4 c. juice from fresh orange	12 slices cinnamon raisin bread, sliced 1 inch thick
1 tbsp. vanilla extract	
2 drops liquid stevia	4 tbsp. butter
1/2 tsp. ground cinnamon	Honey (optional)

In a large bowl, whisk together, eggs, half and half, juice, vanilla, stevia, cinnamon, nutmeg and salt.

Place bread in egg mixture and soak for 30 seconds on each side.

Heat 2 tablespoons of the butter in a large skillet on medium heat. Add the bread to skillet and cook until golden brown, approximately 3 minutes on each side. Repeat, adding butter as needed until all bread is done. Serve with honey, if you desire.

Serve immediately, or place in a preheated oven at 200 F until ready to serve.

** This recipe will use the cinnamon bread in the breads, loaves, and muffins section of this book.

You cannot be lonely if you like the person you are alone with.
- Wayne W. Dyer

HOT AMARANTH CEREAL
WITH CINNAMON APPLES

2 c. water

1 c. amaranth

2 tbsp. coconut oil or butter

1 large apple,
    cored, peeled, and diced

1/2 tsp. cinnamon

1 1/2 tsp. vanilla

4 to 5 drops liquid stevia,
    to taste

On medium-high heat, bring 2 cups water and 1 cup amaranth to a boil. Lower heat to simmer, cover pot and cook for 25 to 30 minutes. Stir to mix remaining water with the amaranth. It should be soft and creamy.

While waiting for amaranth to cook, melt coconut oil or butter in a hot skillet. Add apples and cinnamon. Cook on medium-low heat until soft. Add apple mixture to amaranth. Mix in vanilla and stevia. Combine completely.

** Amaranth has a nutty flavor and is high in protein.

ROASTED CHESTNUTS

1 lb. chestnuts,
    cleaned and dried

A little water for the bottom of
    pan

On flat side of chestnut, cut an x with a knife. Place in shallow baking pan, with 1/8 inch of water.

Bake at 425 F for 30 minutes, or until skins open. Time will depend on size.

Shake pan several times to rotate chestnuts so they cook evenly.

BLUEBERRY SILVER DOLLAR PANCAKES

2 eggs
2 tbsp. coconut oil or butter, melted
2 tbsp. coconut milk
3 drops liquid stevia
1/4 tsp. sea salt

2 Tbsp. coconut flour
1/4 tsp. baking soda
3/4 c. fresh blueberries
1 tbsp. coconut oil to heat in skillet
Whipped cream (optional)

In a small bowl, blend together, eggs, oil, coconut milk, stevia and salt. In a separate bowl, combine coconut flour with baking soda. Mix well.

Mix the coconut flour and baking soda into egg batter. Fold in most of the blueberries, saving some to put on the whipped cream, if using.

Heat one tbsp. of coconut oil in skillet. Using a tbsp., spoon batter onto hot skillet making pancakes about 3 inches in diameter. Batter starts out thick, but will flatten out when cooking. Top with whipped cream and blueberries (optional).

Happiness depends more on the inward disposition of mind, than on outward circumstances.
- Benjamin Franklin

APPLE PECAN CRÊPES

Crêpe Filling:

1 tbsp. butter	1 tsp. cinnamon
1/2 c. pecans, chopped	2 tsp. xylitol
3 Granny Smith apples, cored, peeled, & diced	Whipped cream (optional)

In a large skillet, on medium heat, melt butter and cook pecans until slightly browned.

Add apples, cinnamon and xylitol. Cook until apples are soft.

Keep warm while making crêpes.

Crêpes:

2 eggs	2 tbsp. coconut flour
1/2 tsp. vanilla extract	1/3 c. unsweetened almond milk
1/2 tsp. nutmeg	1 tbsp. butter
1 tsp. xylitol	4 tbsp. cream cheese
1/8 tsp. sea salt	

Blend together eggs, vanilla, nutmeg, xylitol and salt. Mix in coconut flour. Stir in almond milk. Batter will be very thin.

Heat 1 tbsp. butter in a small skillet. Pour 1/4 of the batter into skillet. Immediately rotate skillet until a thin, even layer of batter covers the bottom of the skillet. Crêpe should be about 6 inches in diameter.

Cook until batter is bubbly, and cooked around the edges. Turn and cook the other side. Spread 1 tablespoon of cream cheese on each crêpe.

Put filling on one side of each crêpe and roll up. Top with whipped cream (optional).

HOMEMADE ICE CREAM CONES

2 eggs
1/2 tsp. vanilla extract
1 tsp. cinnamon
1 1/2 tsp. xylitol
1/8 tsp. sea salt

2 tbsp. coconut flour
1/3 c. unsweetened almond milk
1 tbsp. butter

In a blender, blend together, eggs, vanilla, cinnamon, xylitol and salt. Add coconut flour and mix. Blend in almond milk. Batter should be thin.

Heat butter on medium-high heat. Add 1/4 of the batter, rotating the pan so batter forms a thin layer circle.

Cook about 2 minutes, or until batter bubbles. Flip over and cook other side for about 1 minute. Let cool.

Roll up, each circle, to form a cone, beginning with the bottom, and moving to the top. Squeeze the bottom end to seal. Place top end of a 3 inch dixie cup inside the top portion of each cone, to keep it round, and open.

Place cones in the freezer, sealed side down, to hold the form. Keep in freezer until ready to fill with your favorite ice cream.

What you do today is important because you are exchanging a day of your life for it. Let it be something good.
- Unknown

EXTRA RECIPES:

_____

_____

_____

_____

_____

_____

_____

_____

_____

_____

_____

_____

_____

_____

_____

_____

Teri's Gluten-Free & Grain-Free Healthy Recipes

Recipe Index